GO WEST, YOUNG MAN

A FATHER AND SON REDISCOVER AMERICA ON THE OREGON TRAIL

B.J. Hollars

UNIVERSITY OF NEBRASKA PRESS   LINCOLN

Library of Congress
Cataloging-in-Publication Data
Names: Hollars, B. J., author.
Title: Go west, young man: a father
and son rediscover America on the
Oregon Trail / B.J. Hollars.
Other titles: Father and son rediscover
America on the Oregon Trail
Description: Lincoln: University of
Nebraska Press, [2021] | Includes
bibliographical references.
Identifiers: LCCN 2020054617
ISBN 9781496228420 (epub)
ISBN 9781496225900 (paperback)
ISBN 9781496228437 (pdf)
Subjects: LCSH: Hollars, B. J.—Travel—
Oregon National Historic Trail. | Hollars,
B. J.—Family. | Hollars, Henry—Travel—
Oregon National Historic Trail. | Oregon
National Historic Trail—History. |
Northwestern States—Description
and travel. | Automobile travel—
Northwestern States. | Fathers and
sons—Northwestern States. | Fathers and
sons—Oregon National Historic Trail.
Classification: LCC F597 .H73 2021 |
DDC 978—dc23
LC record available at
https://lccn.loc.gov/2020054617

Set in New Baskerville ITC by Laura Buis.
Designed by N. Putens.

For travelers—

past, present, and future.

And for Henry—

wonderer, wanderer, and big-hearted boy.

Look out at the meadow, you can almost see them,

generations dissolved in the bluegrass and hay.

I want to try and be terrific. Even for an hour.

—from Ada Limón's "During the Impossible Age of Everyone"

CONTENTS

ILLUSTRATIONS

ACKNOWLEDGMENTS

Writing this book required a wagon train's worth of support. Thanks to every person we met along the trail, most notably John Bevis, Travis Boley, Randy Brown, Rachel Burr, Roger Castle, Barbara Clark, Mary Cone, Steve Fullmer, Ralph Goldsmith, Gene Hunt, Duane Iles, Ellie Isenhart, John Jarvie, Liz Nakazawa, Karen Nelson, Vance Nelson, Loren Pospisil, Becky Smith, Kale Wuthrich, and Shawneen Wuthrich. Your powerful insights on the past and present allowed this book to be.

Thanks, as always, to my inspiring students. How to thank you for allowing me to live starry-eyed within this book for years?

To my colleagues and friends at the University of Wisconsin–Eau Claire: Dr. Debra Barker, Brett Beach, Chair Erica Benson, Nick Butler, Dr. Dorothy Chan, Dr. Jeff DeGrave, Joanne Erickson, Dean Rodd Freitag, Max Garland, John Hildebrand, Provost Patricia Kleine, Greg Kocken, Allyson Loomis, Jon Loomis, Dean Carmen Manning, Dr. Justin Patchin, Molly Patterson, Chancellor Jim Schmidt, Kim Pickering Schmidt, Patti See, Dr. Asha Sen, Dr. Jason Spraitz, Chair Jan Stirm, Bruce Taylor, Dr. Paul Thomas, and President Kimera Way.

Thanks to Dr. Karen Havholm and the Office of Research and Sponsored Programs at the University of Wisconsin–Eau Claire, whose travel support proved vital to this project. Thanks, too, for the support provided by the University of Wisconsin–Eau Claire Academic Affairs Professional Development Program.

To the Eau Claire writing community and, in particular, early reader Jim Alf. But also, Tom Giffey, Kyran Hamill, Rebecca Mennecke, Nick Meyer, and Mike Paulus. And to the well-wishers too: Mike Felton, Matt Larson, Todd Leavitt, Jim McDougall, Josh Miller, and oh so many more.

Thank you to the Wait! What? Writers and to Eric Rasmussen, in particular.

To Sarah Johnson and Serena Wagner of Odd Brand Strategy for the mapmaking and for creating a better world.

To the University of Nebraska Press family, and especially to my eagle-eyed copyeditor, Elizabeth Gratch.

And finally, to my family—looking forward to the journey ahead.

AUTHOR'S NOTE

While writing a book about the Oregon Trail isn't nearly as difficult as crossing it, indeed, it has its challenges. Part of the trouble is that the trail's a mirage of sorts—simultaneously there but not there, viewable but only when you know where to look. To a great extent this book was written thanks to the people who showed me where to direct my eyes, dozens of interviews conducted both on scene and in person. In a few instances I interviewed people on several occasions, then, for readability purposes, incorporated their comments into a single scene. It's worth noting that my number one interviewee wasn't an interviewee at all but my son and sidekick, then-six-year-old Henry. While I like to think our banter is always as delightful as depicted herein, I'll admit that on a few occasions, by way of language selection, I claimed fatherly privilege and amped up our delightfulness just a smidgen.

My primary sources came in many forms, though mainly trail journals. There's no better way to get inside the hearts and minds of nineteenth-century overland emigrants than by reading their own accounts. Thankfully, several online repositories—including the Oregon-California Trails Association's collections—provide a wealth of trail journals available to the public.

For a complete list of sources, I refer you to the bibliography at the end of this book. For now I'll offer thanks to the authors and historians whom I relied upon most frequently, those who became fellow travelers in my own personal wagon train: Merrill Mattes, Irene

Paden, John Unruh, Gregory Franzwa, Dee Brown, Roxanne Dunbar-Ortiz, and Rinker Buck. I wouldn't have made it a mile without you.

This book would not have been possible without the work of those who've come before. In many instances I employed direct quotations from trail journals and historical scholarship to bolster and support my own work. For readability purposes I often refer to individuals and historians broadly rather than credit them by name within the text itself. Make no mistake: these individuals deserve full credit for their words; citations are available in the notes section of this book.

When writing of America's first inhabitants, I have taken a cue from similar books by using the phrases *Native American* as well as *indigenous people.* In a few quotations the phrase *American Indian* is also employed. Additionally, every effort was made to reference specific tribal nations when appropriate and verifiable.

It's important to note too—as I do in chapter 4—that I am far from the ideal conveyer of the many Native American portions of this story. White writers such as me need to do a far better job of elevating, centering, and amplifying indigenous voices rather than try to tell this history ourselves. Though my efforts in this regard remain wholly insufficient, I have tried to rely upon Native American voices, both past and present, to offer a more complete and more accurate portrayal of this story. A visit to Tamástslikt Cultural Institute in Pendleton, Oregon—which provides a tribal perspective of western expansionism—fundamentally altered my understanding of this history. Please visit if you can.

Finally, to the Oregon Trail–loving rut nuts, I beg your pardon in advance. This book was never intended to be a complete history, nor would I be brash enough to attempt such a feat. The ruts are too deep, the routes too plentiful.

As the emigrant expression goes, I "saw the elephant" while writing this book.

Hell, this book is the elephant.

GO WEST, YOUNG MAN

1. B.J. and Henry's summer 2018 road trip route. Courtesy of Odd Brand Strategies.

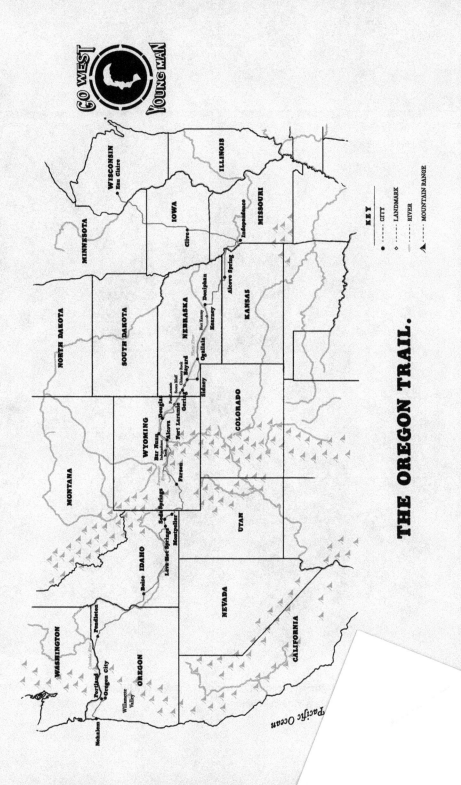

THE OREGON TRAIL.

2. Conestoga wagon on Oregon Trail. National Archives and Records Administration, via Wikimedia Commons.

Prologue

There are two types of journeys: the ones where you're running away from something and the ones where you're running toward something. As Henry and I began hashing out details to retrace the Oregon Trail, it seemed we were running in opposite directions. While I was running us away from the trappings of twenty-first-century technology (the abundance of screen time was altering our family dynamic), Henry was running us toward an America he could hardly imagine: the Wild West. No matter that the West hadn't been "wild" in over a century; for him—based on the cartoons he'd seen—it remained the wildest place possible.

Which is to say, we both had our reasons for this trip. Mine was fueled by fear of missing out on our time together, his by way of the high-octane enthusiasm that only a six-year-old knows. As my world contracted, his expanded, and he couldn't wait to see all of it.

And I couldn't wait to show it to him.

However, a part of me worried that we'd already missed our window for such a trip. That when he viewed me now, he didn't see his best bud in the whole wide world but his buzzkill of a father: the chastiser, the enforcer, the furrow-browed dad. We both longed for the other guy, but how to lure that other guy back? How far would I have to run to find the me who'd vanished?

In addition to strengthening my relationship with my son (and perhaps rediscovering a bit of myself), I also set my sights on an objective for which I was even less qualified: rediscovering America. Of course, such a claim borders on the absurd. After all, what writer would be foolhardy enough to try to capture America's story by way of a road trip?

John Steinbeck, for one, who in the fall of 1960 drove his camper truck cross-country to answer the question: "What are Americans like today?"[1] Fully aware of his daunting charge, Steinbeck solicited the help of an unlikely sidekick, a French poodle named Charley.

"In establishing contact with strange people, Charley is my ambassador," Steinbeck wrote. "I release him, and he drifts toward the objective, or rather to whatever the objective may be preparing for dinner." By breaking down social barriers, Charley more than earned his keep.

"A child can do the same thing," Steinbeck added, "but a dog is better."

Maybe in most cases, but John Steinbeck never met Henry Hollars.

Personable, big-hearted, and nearly as handsome as his father, I knew Henry would bring his own unique skill sets to our two-person wagon train. Most important of all, his unrelenting curiosity. Of the many sentences that leave his mouth, the majority begin with a *who, what, when, where,* or *why.* When I offer answers, he responds with more questions. It's as charming as it is maddening.

"I know *you* think the world is round," he'll say, "but how do you know for sure?"

"Because . . . science!" I'll stammer.

Which is my roundabout way of saying that I've got much to learn too. And not just about science but about history. And geography. And art. And meteorology. And cooking. And tire changing. And oil changing. And the importance of staking down tents. Our country is ripe with opportunities for discovery; the hard part is how to make sense of it all.

In this regard even John Steinbeck struggled. When trying to draw conclusions on 1960s America, he wrote: "It would be pleasant to be able to say of my travels with Charley, 'I went out to find the truth about my country and I found it.' And then it would be such a simple matter to set down my findings and lean back comfortably with a fine sense of having discovered truths and taught them to my readers. I wish it were that easy."

Though perhaps what most makes us Americans is our refusal to conform to a one-size-fits-all model. We are more complex, more multifaceted, and—if the twenty-four-hour news cycle is to be believed—more divisive as a result of our diversity of thought. It is the price we pay for being more melting pot than mold.

Despite twenty-first-century travelers' various motives for retracing the trail, according to the late Gregory Franzwa, the granddaddy of modern trail scholars, we can all expect at least one shared outcome: by trip's end modern travelers will become endowed "with a new and more intense feeling for American history."[2] I sure hope so. Because I want desperately to feel more for my country. To reconnect with a place I've never left but still somehow feel disconnected from. While a part of me hopes to reaffirm my convictions for what I believe America to be, another part strives to do the harder thing: unsaddle my high horse, stand down from my soapbox, and allow a difference in opinion to serve as the opening salvo to a conversation rather than the final word.

Mapless and guideless, I am in search of a middle ground that may or may not still exist in America. Perhaps I am being woefully optimistic even to try. But so were the overland emigrants when they packed their lives into wagons and made the two-thousand-plus-mile trek to the Willamette Valley.

Their journey came with its risks, as does everything.

"Dad," Henry said one night as we lay in bed dreaming of our journey. "What do you think we'll find out west anyway?"

Where to begin? Ourselves? Our country? A little of both?

"Everything," I said at last. "If we're lucky, we'll find everything."

"Everything," he repeated. "Yeah, okay. Let's look for that."

Staring at his ceiling, my mind leaped suddenly to a quotation from author Robert Louis Stevenson, a man who knew a thing or two about adventure.

"Old and young," Stevenson wrote, "we are all on our last cruise."

It leaves with or without us.

No waiting for favorable winds.

3. Henry's illustration of our grand arrival at McDonald's. Courtesy of the author.

1 The Jumping-Off Point

> For what do they brave the desert, the wilderness, the savage, the snowy precipices of the Rocky Mountains, the weary summer march, the storm-drenched bivouac and the gnawing of famine? . . . This migration of more than a thousand persons in one body to Oregon wears an aspect of insanity.
>
> —Horace Greeley, 1843

THURSDAY, JUNE 7
WEATHER: WARM
RATIONS: FILLING
EAU CLAIRE WI → CLIVE IA

On a dark winter night six months prior to embarking upon the greatest adventure of our lives, I woke to my six-year-old's screams.

Stumbling over a minefield of action figures and race cars, I made my way to Henry's bed.

"Hey, buddy," I said, "what hurts?"

He clasped his hands to his thighs.

"Legs, huh?"

More screaming.

Doctor that I'm not, I began offering a smorgasbord of half-baked diagnoses: broken leg, fractured leg, broken and fractured leg. As I began to awaken more fully, I came to a slightly more reasonable explanation. Maybe his legs were asleep.

"You're going to be fine," I said, massaging his thighs.

His wails argued otherwise.

I called in reinforcements, my wife, Meredith, who at 2:00 a.m. had become a steely-eyed Florence Nightingale.

"What do we got?" I asked. "Broken leg?"

She didn't dignify my joke with a response. Instead, she took one look at him and then moved to the bathroom closet, our well-stocked apothecary shop overflowing with the usual fare: antacids, calamine lotion, cough drops.

Returning to Henry's bedside, she poured him a shot of liquid pain reliever, which he downed heartily.

"Problem solved?" I asked.

As if to prove it, Henry was back to snoring within minutes.

"What the hell just happened?" I asked as we returned to our bedroom.

"Growing pains," Meredith said, reaching for the sheets.

"Growing pains?"

She nodded. "Our little boy's growing up."

Never in my wildest dreams had I imagined my firstborn's growth rendered so dramatically. Wasn't growth supposed to be an unobservable process? A metamorphosis so gradual that it couldn't be seen in real time?

Technically, we hadn't seen it; we'd heard it. But hearing it was enough. His screams served as a wake-up call to a future I wasn't ready to face.

"So what do we do?" I asked. "How do we slow life down?"

"We can't," she said, closing her eyes.

Which sounded like a challenge to me.

★ ★ ★

We might've chosen another trail—Lewis and Clark's, the Appalachian, the Pacific Crest—but we chose the Oregon Trail, in part, because of its historical allure. We wanted to see the route that had stitched our country together. A stitching that took place at the hands of the overland emigrants whose travels helped transform territories into states and, in doing so, gave "America the Beautiful" lyricist Katharine Lee Bates the chance to pen a line as poetic as it was geographically accurate: "from sea to shining sea."

The country grew, but not without revealing its darker side: one reeking of land grabs, cultural genocide, and the bloodshed of tens of thousands of indigenous people. The story of westward expansion is so chocked full of exploitation that we dare not look away. But facing it, too, can prove problematic. Especially for a guy like me, whose surface-level understanding of this epoch in history doesn't come close to grasping the depth of the wound wrought upon this country. A wound that is now a scar, and a scar that, for many indigenous people, is in the form of the Oregon Trail itself.

Too often, history reads like a game of telephone—stories passed on and on and changing as they go. This feels particularly true for the history of the American West, ground zero for many of America's trespasses. Today most citizens acknowledge how American expansionism directly contributed to the exploitation of Native Americans. We know the broad strokes at least. Or we think we do. But the devil is in the details. And when it comes to history, the details are often the first facts to go missing.

How different America might be if Katharine Lee Bates's lyrics offered a more accurate depiction. If, on that fateful day in 1893 that inspired it all, she'd peered down from the top of Pikes Peak to see more than the country's natural beauty.[1] What if her lyrics had captured not only the "amber waves of grain" and the "purple mountain majesties" but also those people who were no longer visible in the Colorado wilderness below? Where were the Apaches and the Arapahos and the Cheyennes? Admittedly, it would have been the more difficult song to write. But today, over 125 years after "America the Beautiful" first rang out, it's evident that America's overdue for a new song or an updated song or a truer song at least.

Throughout our trip Henry and I will regularly reflect on the complexities of the American West, but admittedly, our grappling with this history (and our place within it) was but one reason we struck out in that direction. The other was a bit more arbitrary.

It began on Christmas Eve 2017, when then-five-year-old Henry and his three-year-old sister, Eleanor, left the church pews to take their places among the children's choir. They dragged their feet every step of the way, Eleanor sticking close to her big brother, whom she assumed had some sense of what was occurring. He didn't. Nevertheless, they stood at the front of the sanctuary to offer us parishioners a mercifully mumbled rendition of "We Three Kings."

Yet in the midst of their mumbles, Henry's voice turned suddenly clear. He'd reached the one line of the song he actually knew, which he belted out at full volume.

"Westward leading, still proceeding . . . Guide us to thy perfect light . . ."

Eleanor shot him a lifted eyebrow, astonished that of all the words in the world, her brother had—in this instance—stumbled upon the correct ones. For Henry the miracle hardly registered. Hands stuffed in his pockets, he was back to lip-synching within seconds, his wasp's nest of curls springing with every bob of his head.

At the conclusion of the final note, the congregation burst into cheers. Since no one vomited or fell off the stage, the performance was deemed a success. The children retreated to their parents, Eleanor taking her place on my lap while Henry shimmied between friends in the front pew.

For the remainder of the service, we learned, once more, about baby Jesus in the manger. But my thoughts were on other babies. Two, in particular, who were no longer babies at all. As Eleanor army crawled beneath the pews, I kept my eyes on the curly head of hair directly ahead of me. In my mind I heard the echo of the song: *Westward leading, still proceeding . . . Guide us to thy perfect light . . .*

Call it what you will—serendipity, divine intervention, a father's overly literal reading of lyrics. Whatever it was, to my ear it sounded like a clarion call.

One that pointed us toward the glorious American West.

I am hardly the first to romanticize it.

As one scholar notes, throughout the nineteenth century America's western frontier "was generally presented to Americans as Xanadu, a mind-expanding experience as well as a semi-magical

4. Albert Bierstadt's *Emigrants Crossing the Plains, or The Oregon Trail*, 1867. Butler Institute of American Art, via Wikimedia Commons.

place symbolizing opportunity, civilization over savagery, predestination, material progress and freedom."[2] For prospective emigrants it seemed a wonderland beyond compare, one where gold and glory could be easily obtained simply by pointing oneself in the right direction.

If such mythmaking wasn't enticing enough, German American painter Albert Bierstadt's 1869 oil on canvas painting, *Emigrants Crossing the Plains, or The Oregon Trail*, provided a visual representation of the West sure to make Americans' imaginations run wild. Following a land surveying trip in 1859, Bierstadt returned to his easel to share what he'd seen: a pristine landscape primed for exploration and discovery. A mere glimpse of the glowing sunset through the tall trees, coupled with the emigrants and their meandering livestock, was an inspiration for later waves of travelers. His paintings earned the admiration of Lt. Col. George Armstrong Custer, who, while peering out at the Wichita Mountains from atop his horse, remarked that the view was "worthy the brush of a [Frederic Edwin] Church, a Bierstadt."[3]

Bierstadt had his detractors ("What has he done but twist and skew and distort and discolor and belittle and be-pretty this whole doggoned country," grumbled a geologist who took umbrage with Bierstadt's mountains),[4] though most people fell under Bierstadt's hypnotic depictions, romanticized as they were.

On the literary front Henry David Thoreau managed much the same work. Long fascinated by the West and perhaps tiring of a life-time spent in and around Concord, Thoreau famously proclaimed, "Eastward I go only by force; but westward I go free."[5] Yet due to illness, Thoreau only ever got a taste of that freedom, dying within a year of his westernmost trip to Minnesota.

Seated in that pew, I didn't want to repeat Thoreau's mistake. If I, too, wanted to experience that rumored-to-exist western freedom, then what was I waiting for? What but routine was pinning me to this place?

The answer: technology.

In the preceding years I, like so many of my generation, had fallen face first into the trappings of twenty-first-century existence. One in which my smartphone doubled as my safety blanket, disincentivizing any authentic experience and replacing it with a secondhand glimpse of somebody else's. Why go through all the trouble of living, after all, when you can simply watch somebody else do it? In recent months I'd grown despondent at the prospect of watching my life slip through my scrolling fingers. I'd become worried, too, that if I didn't make a fundamental change to my lifestyle, I'd barely be living at all.

Though I worried about my own quality of life, I was far more concerned about the long-term consequences of technology on my relationship with my children. What if there came a day when my son or daughter only recognized me in the glow of a screen? And equally terrifying, what if I only recognized them similarly? What if they observed all my hours squandered on screen time and decided to follow suit?

I was particularly worried about Henry, who'd reached the age in which my attention-fractured state had become noticeable. Sometimes, between swipes, I'd glance his way to notice him noticing me. Shamefacedly, I'd pocket my phone, then try a little harder to remain present.

Though I recognized the problem, the solution seemed less clear.

How to do what Thoreau had done right and try to live deliberately?

Following the service we bundled into our coats and gloves and braced ourselves for the single-digit temperatures that awaited us. Pushing the wooden doors wide, we made a break for it, me holding Eleanor while Henry and Meredith tromped through the freshly fallen snow.

We buckled up, our teeth chattering in the frozen air. Glancing Henry in the rearview, I was grateful to still recognize his face.

This was the moment I began to live deliberately.

"Hey Henry," I said. "You want to take a trip?"

He paused, considering it for all of two seconds.

"Sure," he agreed. "Why not?"

★ ★ ★

Our decision to travel west was hardly as high stakes as the emigrants who came before. Embarking on such an adventure, complete with the luxuries of today, all but ensured our safe passage. Even in the off chance that the going did get tough, we were always just a U-turn away from turning tail.

But for the Martin Baker Gay family of Springfield, Illinois—and tens of thousands of emigrants like them—the decision to trade in the life they knew for the one they didn't had the potential to cost them life, limb, and livelihood. As Martha Gay Masterson later recalled, when her father broached the idea of traveling to Oregon in 1850, her mother, Ann, was strongly opposed.

"She begged father to give up the notion," Masterson wrote, "but he could not."[6]

Given nineteenth-century patriarchal norms, Ann was left with little choice, as was true of many westward-traveling women. As one scholar noted, "Women were part of the journey because their fathers, husbands, and brothers had determined to go. They went West because there was no other way for them *not* to go once the decision was made."[7]

As a result, many wives were forced to endure an experience quite different than that of their husbands. Perhaps the greatest difference was that an estimated 20 percent of women underwent the most dangerous journey of their lives while pregnant. In the event that disease, accidents, and limited food and water didn't prove challenging enough, one in five women were also walking a dozen or more miles a day while trying to bring a child to term.

To say that nineteenth-century husbands and wives didn't always see eye to eye on the matter of westward travel would be an understatement. "If ever there was a time when men and women turned their psychic energies toward opposite visions," one scholar wrote, "the overland journey was that time."[8]

Shortly after Ann "reluctantly consented" to the journey, Martin gathered his eleven children, including then twelve-year-old Martha, and shared the wonders that awaited them: the Pacific Ocean, the Columbia River, and the tree-filled Willamette Valley.[9]

"He then explained the hardships and dangers," Masterson continued, "the sufferings and the dreary long days we would journey on and on before we would reach Oregon."[10]

As Masterson recalled, her father then asked her and her siblings if they wanted to go. "We rather thought we wanted to stay with our school friends and our societies," Masterson wrote. "But children were expected to do as their parents said in those days and father said we must come."[11]

Overriding the other twelve members of his family, Martin began overseeing preparations for their journey. Throughout 1850 and 1851 all attempts to persuade Martin to reconsider fell on deaf ears. When warned by friends that they would surely be killed by Native Americans, Masterson recalled her father assuring them that "he was not as much alarmed about the Indians as many other obstacles we might encounter: the swollen streams, the cyclones and dangerous roads, the snow in the mountains, sickness, suffering for water, shortage of fuel and other privations."[12]

Since Martin could not be dissuaded, their friends and relatives had no choice but to bid them safe travels. The family home was sold, their possessions distributed, and following a farewell sermon, on the morning of April 10, 1851, they prepared to embark on their adventure.

"All places of business and the schools were closed during the forenoon, and everybody came to say goodbye to us," Masterson remembered. "From early morning till ten o'clock they came. The house and yard and streets were crowded with people. Friends and schoolmates were crying all around us."[13]

Following the final hugs and handshakes, the covered wagon rolled across the yard and headed west. "We took a long last look at it all," Masterson wrote, "then closed our eyes on the scene and moved forward."[14]

★ ★ ★

One hundred and sixty-seven years later, when Henry and I strike out, no farewell sermons are preached on our behalf. Business continues as usual. No tears are tendered or received. Though, admittedly, I come pretty close to giving my own tear ducts a flush when saying goodbye to our own people. Henry offers a big hug to Mom, followed by a tackle in the grass for Eleanor. Never one to miss an opportunity to contribute to chaos, Cici, our Chihuahua-spaniel, bids us farewell with an enthusiasm typically reserved for intruding postal workers.

None of them have ever looked more beautiful. The afternoon light catches them in a perfect prism, one that transforms even our snaggle-toothed hound into the winner of Westminster.

It's not too late to call it off, I think. *Not too late to stay right here in your lovely home with your lovely family and enjoy a carefree and unencumbered summer.*

But it is too late. I've been planning this trip for months—had even prepaid two weeks' worth of campsites. To turn back before we even started was a cowardice I couldn't bear.

"Good luck," Meredith says as we break from our hug, cleaving our family in two.

"We'll be fine," I say.

"You sure?" she asks.

"As sure as sure can be."

Buckling into our newly rented 2018 Jeep Compass, we begin rolling in reverse down the drive.

It's happening. We're doing it.

Only we're not. There's a problem with the car. When I put the Jeep in drive, it just keeps rolling backward, wholly unresponsive to my frantic taps on the accelerator. My eyes scan the touchscreen to my right, which has more buttons than a Boeing Airbus.

What in the world's going on?

Then it hits me: amid all our farewells, I forgot to press the ignition button. It's a problem no nineteenth-century emigrant ever had to face. Upon pressing the button, the Jeep roars to life.

Meredith's jaw drops. "Did you really forget to start the car?"

"We'll be fine!" I shout, pressing down hard on the accelerator.

As harbingers go, four flat tires and a lightning bolt couldn't have sent a clearer message: *Turn. Back. Now.*

★ ★ ★

We've barely made it five miles when Henry, without a hint of irony, peers out the window and says, "The world sure looks different out here."

"Buddy, we drive this way all the time."

"Oh," he says. "Well . . . I guess the grass just looks taller."

I've got to give him credit for trying. For months I'd been training him on the lost art of looking out the window, promising that once we ventured deep enough along the trail, he'd see a world he never knew existed: snowcapped mountains, endless vistas, and a sky stretching just shy of forever.

"But that reminds me," I say, "today I saw something pretty cool out the window myself."

"What?"

"I was picking up the rental car when I saw this dump truck—"

"Cool!"

"That's not even the cool part. The cool part was the bumper sticker on the back of the dump truck. It was a slogan of sorts." I lift my hand to the air to accentuate every word. "'Make every mile a memory.'"

"Make every mile a memory?"

"Yeah. I think we should give that a try."

"Like . . . *every* mile?"

"Well, as many as we can."

His mind sets to spinning.

"But . . . what if there are miles when nothing really happens?"

"I think the point is we should make an effort to—"

"Or what if it's just a lot of boring old road? Or desert? Or like a mixture of road and desert and not much else . . . ?"

When at last we run out of hypotheticals, Henry agrees to give it a try. To the best of his ability, he will make every memorable mile a memory. To prove it, he reaches for his black-and-white composition book and his crayons, then gets to work preserving the wholly familiar terrain just beyond the Jeep's window.

Forty-five minutes later, while passing Pepin, Wisconsin, I tell him to make a memory.

"Of what?"

"This is where Laura Ingalls Wilder lived," I explain. "You know, from the *Little House* books?"

"So . . . I'm supposed to make a memory of what?"

I sigh.

"Just think of it: when she was a little girl, she and her family packed their wagon and headed west. Just like we're doing now. For all we know, they crossed these very hills. Isn't that amazing?"

He's not sure if it is or it isn't.

Meanwhile, I'm borderline giddy by the prospect of following in such famous wagon ruts. And I'm fascinated, too, by Wilder's description of her father's rationale for leaving Wisconsin for the West.

"Pa said there were too many people in the Big Woods now," Wilder wrote. "Quite often Laura heard the ringing thud of an ax which was not Pa's ax, or the echo of a shot that did not come from his gun. The path that went by the little home had become a road. Almost every day Laura and Mary stopped their playing and stared in surprise at a wagon slowly creaking by on that road."[15]

Wilder's depiction of the rapidly expanding American frontier—while riveting to millions of readers—leaves something to be desired for kids like Henry. A product of his time, he's looking for a little more speed in the plot, and unfortunately for him, the book plods at a wagon's pace.

"Well, *I* think it's pretty cool," I try one last time. "I mean, just imagine a kid not much older than you riding across this prairie . . ."

He'd rather imagine most anything else and, for the next couple of hours, does. Returning to his composition book, he draws a parade of monsters, all of whom have an elaborate backstory and none of which involves the Oregon Trail.

We cross the Mississippi River in the early evening, thundering along Interstate 90 and leaving half a dozen small towns in our wake. They appear built from the same blueprint: there is the gas station, the restaurant, the post office, and the stoplight. On occasion we spot a municipal swimming pool—each of which causes Henry to claw at the window.

"Can't we stop?" he pleads as we watch the cannonballing boys hurling themselves from the diving boards.

"Not today," I say. "But don't worry! We've got all kinds of fun stuff in our future—"

The words barely leave my lips before a bird crashes beak-first into our windshield.

The *thunk* resembles a well-struck bongo drum.

I manage to keep from swerving, though I'm shaken by the black smear of feathers now flopped to the road just behind us.

"Was that a . . . bird?" Henry asks.

"I believe so."

"And we killed it?"

"I'm afraid so."

Henry turns silent.

"So," he says at last, "want me to make that a memory?"

I shoot him a grin in the rearview.

"Zip it."

★ ★ ★

We're hardly the first wagon train to get off to a rocky start. In fact, a good number of emigrants never made it beyond their front yards. Just packing a wagon was worthy of commendation; why risk some future failure? Even those who endured as far as the jumping-off points—Independence, Missouri; St. Joseph, Missouri; and Council Bluffs, Iowa; to name a few—were hardly guaranteed to log many more miles beneath their wheels. Sickness was prevalent in the camps and sometimes long before.

And sickness, of course, was just one of many ways to die on the trail. Let's not forget stampedes or snakebites or lightning strikes. Or being crushed by a wagon wheel. Or drowning in a current. Or accidentally shooting oneself with one's gun (which happened with astonishing regularity). By comparison, our own inauspicious start was nothing more than a bird-sized speed bump.

Still, Henry and I decided to drown our sorrows in the bottom of a bag of fast food.

"You pick the place," I say.

I know his answer before it leaves his mouth.

"McDonald's!"

"Buddy, I'm not sure there are any McDonald's coming up—"

"Right there!" he says, pointing to the exit for Albert Lea, Minnesota.

5. Embarking upon our first McDonald's, Albert Lea, Minnesota. Courtesy of the author.

Sighing, I turn off the highway and onto Happy Trails Lane, which seems appropriate, given our journey.

"I wonder if the pioneers stopped here," Henry ponders as we park at the Trail's Travel Center.

With the fortitude of a well-trained bloodhound, Henry leads me toward McDonald's. He knows the drill: Happy Meal for him, a couple of dollar menu items for me. We place our order, bide our time taste-testing every soft drink at the soda fountain, and then, when our number is called, sidle up to the stools to partake in America's favorite pastime: shoving food into our mouth holes. I gobble my way through a bagful of burgers, then wash them down with a miniature bucket of high-fructose corn syrup.

Henry, meanwhile, makes short work of his Happy Meal—a food concept foreign to the original overland emigrants, for whom a happy meal was any meal that didn't induce cholera. What the emigrants lacked in French fries and chicken nuggets they made up for with their own dietary staples: bread, bacon, coffee, beans, rice, and, when the hunting was good, a slab of buffalo meat. There were indulgences, too (no wagon train was complete without a barrel of whiskey), though given the space limitations of a covered wagon, fondue pots and chocolate fountains were typically left at home.

Following our meal, we top off the gas tank, empty our bladders, then take once more to the road.

"How much longer?" Henry asks, re-buckling.

"One hundred and fifty miles to the motel in Clive, Iowa," I report.

"Is that far?"

"Nah," I say.

Which is the truth compared to what's coming.

★ ★ ★

The rain begins to fall as the sun sets over northern Iowa. Yet before I can flick on the wipers, the Jeep does it for me. I'm taken aback by such forward behavior. Who does this Jeep think it is? I'm led to two equally chilling conclusions: either the car is secretly being driven by robots or the ghost of that bird we killed has infiltrated the electronic control system. All I know for sure is that our Jeep—complete with every bell and whistle imaginable—views me more as a passenger than a driver.

Sure, you think *you're in control,* a voice whispers through the air vents, *but why not sit back and let me do the driving* . . .

It's a tempting offer. And for a guy who's used to driving a 2008 Ford Focus (one that occasionally requires a Fred Flintstone–inspired foot push), the prospect of ceding control to my robot overlords seems worthy of full consideration.

But I refuse to hit cruise control and let the robots win. And it's a good thing. Because not even the smartest robot (or the most vindictive ghost bird) could have handled what happens next.

It starts as a minor inconvenience: a semitruck driver riding my bumper in the passing lane.

No matter, I think, *I'll just get in the right lane.*

I check my blind spot and make my move, assuming that will be the end of it.

But it is not. Upon peering in the rearview, I'm surprised to find that rather than pass me, the trucker's tailing me instead.

Well that's odd . . .

Adding to the drama is the trucker's newfound fascination with flashing his headlights, all but blinding me in the process.

Now, I've read enough urban legends to know how this one ends—there's a killer in my back seat and the trucker's trying to warn me. Though my more logical self (the one that doesn't believe in ghost birds) knows that's impossible. There's no killer in the back seat, just Henry and a Styrofoam cooler full of snacks.

What an asshole, I think, glancing at the trucker in the rearview for a second time.

Yet my grumbles fail to put me at ease given that the alleged asshole is packing forty tons of weight in the back of his freighter. I'd already seen what a car could do to a bird, and I dared not guess what a semi could do to a car.

Finally, after a short eternity, the trucker eases back into the left lane. But even then, he refuses to leave, preferring to keep perfect pace alongside me.

"Um . . . Dad," Henry says, glancing up from his composition book, "is everything okay?"

"Everything's great," I say, sweating.

When at last I muster the courage to glance over, I see a silhouette of a man gesticulating wildly in my direction.

"What?" I shout. "What do you want from me?"

The trucker points to my headlights, which my robot overlords have failed to illuminate.

"Oh," I say sheepishly, "well that, obviously."

I turn on the lights, and the road reappears before me.

One last glance to my left reveals the trucker's silhouette. He gives me a thumbs up, a hearty wave, and in his final act of kindness, speeds off to spare me more embarrassment.

"Let that be a lesson to you," I tell Henry.

"What's that?" he asks.

"Truckers rule."

★ ★ ★

If National Lampoon's *Vacation* has taught us anything, it's that nothing bonds (or breaks) a family better than a good, old-fashioned road trip. Yet for America's nineteenth-century overland emigrants, bonding was beside the point. Reaching their destination safely was the point, and their odds increased mightily once they'd assembled a competent wagon train.

For Henry and me, assembling our train was pretty straightforward: we invited two people, and those people were us. Of course, such an arrangement would have never worked for the westward-bound emigrants, whose wagon trains required members with diversified skill sets.

Which raised the question: what, besides curiosity and a kindly disposition, could Henry bring to our trip?

We had discussed it as a family one morning over French toast.

"What do you mean 'bring'?" Henry asked.

"You know, like what skills can you offer?"

He reached for the syrup.

"Umm . . . I can punch people?"

"I'm not sure there's going to be a lot of opportunity for that," I said. "What else?"

"I mean I can punch *robbers*," he clarified.

"You think robbers are going to be a major problem for us?"

"Better safe than sorry," he shrugged.

"You're a good listener," Meredith suggested. "And you're nice to people."

"Yeah," agreed Eleanor, "and you can pour syrup in your cereal!"

(Then she proceeded to prove that she could too.)

"Let's keep thinking about it," I said. "I know you've got tons to offer."

As breakfast wound down and Henry and my wife started in on their daily ritual of searching for lost shoes, lost backpacks, and lost homework, I kept my attention on the question at hand.

What skills could Henry bring on our journey?

I thought back to a trip we'd taken a few years earlier, when four-year-old Henry had accompanied me to a book festival. It was our first weekend away, and in order to make the most of it, following my reading, we returned to the hotel for a night of revelry. By which I mean we settled in for a night of eating a bucket of ice while watching cable cartoons. We found the cartoons, no problem, but the ice machine was another matter.

We struck out for the hotel ice machine shortly after sunset, wandering the various floors to no avail. Downtrodden as we were, we didn't give up hope. And our stick-to-itiveness paid off when, a few minutes later, we came upon a stranger holding his own empty ice bucket.

"No luck?" I asked.

"Nothing yet," he said.

"Well," I promised, "if we find it first, we'll let you know."

"Back at ya," he agreed.

The stranger went one way, and we went the other, and at last—after a lot of backtracking and zigzagging and wrong turns—we eventually found the elusive ice machine in some out-of-the-way nook.

Henry ran toward it, placing the bucket beneath its wide mouth and reveling in the machine's thunderous churning.

Mission (almost) accomplished.

We were halfway back to those cartoons when Henry paused mid-step.

"Uh-oh."

"Uh-oh what?"

"What about the guy?" he asked.

"The ice bucket guy?"

He nodded. "We have to find him."

And so, at Henry's insistence, we continued wandering the hotel's corridors.

"You know, he probably found it on his own," I tried. "In fact, I bet he's back in his room enjoying a bucket of ice right now."

Henry wouldn't hear of it. We'd promised, hadn't we? And what kind of people would we be if we broke our promise to that ice-loving stranger we'd just met?

As we trudged up a stairwell, I explained that sometimes people just say things with no intention of following through. It's not a lie, exactly, merely friendly conversation.

"And besides, it's just ice," I reminded. "It's not like we promised him a kidney."

"There he is!" Henry interrupted.

Sure enough, there was our stranger flagging us down from the opposite end of the hall.

"You guys find it?" he asked, hustling toward us.

"We did!" I agreed.

Suddenly, we peered into our ice buckets to learn that in the time we spent searching for one another, our ice had melted to water. Thankfully, it was nothing a second visit to the ice machine couldn't fix.

"Yes!" Henry said as he skipped down the hall, his fresh batch of ice in tow. "We found him!"

We had. And a little melted ice was a small price to pay given what else I'd found that night: my perfect travel companion. Someone to remind me that the wagon train always comes first. And that one act of kindness begets another.

* * *

To say that I was naive to the trials ahead would be giving me too much credit. I was woefully ignorant to the challenges that lingered on the horizon. Worse still, I was so supercharged on enthusiasm that it was impossible for me to see the error of my ways. From the first mile I had my rose-colored glasses so firmly affixed to my face that all I could see was wonder. Which is a fine way to live for a little while, right up until reality sets in.

After covering some three hundred miles throughout that first evening, reality at last set in. Over the past twelve hours Henry had survived both his last day of kindergarten and his first day on the road—a one-two punch that left him reeling.

At a few minutes past 9:00 p.m., Henry dragged himself into a motel lobby in Clive, Iowa, then collapsed into the nearest chair. He was so tired he didn't even look for the ice machine. Instead, he turned his attention to the TV, perking up slightly when he noticed it playing our favorite movie, *The Great Outdoors*. A slaphappy Henry cackled as John Candy failed to persuade a couple of black bears to get off the roof of his station wagon.

"Hey," I whispered, "if we keep enough food in the car, maybe that could be us!"

"I hope so," Henry yawned.

Though we'd already successfully driven through three states (Wisconsin, Minnesota, and Iowa), upon receiving the key card, we still managed to get lost en route to our room. When we eventually spotted it tucked beneath a stairwell, we entered to find the last bed we'd see for days. From there on out we'd be roughing it like the emigrants. Well, like the emigrants if they had a North Face tent and a campsite with running water.

The room was adequate, though nothing to write home about.

Twenty-four hours later—when the storm struck—I'd have given the world for it.

6. Henry's illustration of Ralph and the mules. Courtesy of the author.

2

Stubborn as Mules

One afternoon, when the sun seemed to be about three hours high, and we were traveling along at ox-team gait, over a level prairie, John East, a good, honest man, also from Missouri, who was walking and driving his team, was told that we were then crossing the Missouri line, whereupon, he turned about facing the east, pulled off his slouched hat, and waving it above his head said, "Farewell to America!"

—Jesse Applegate, 1843

FRIDAY, JUNE 8
WEATHER: SIZZLING
RATIONS: INDEPENDENCE'S FINEST HOTDOGS, CHERRY PHOSPHATES
CLIVE IA → INDEPENDENCE MO → ALCOVE SPRING KS → DONIPHAN NE

At 7:51 a.m. Henry informs me he's ready for lunch.

"Buddy," I say, glancing him in the rearview, "we just had breakfast an hour ago."

"An *entire* hour ago," he agrees.

All those bagels back at our hotel have since become ancient history. Those carbs have been spent, Henry informs me, and what he needs now is something of the ham and cheese on cracker variety. He nods to the Lunchables in the cooler to his left.

"That's lunch," I explain. "Not second breakfast."

"Call it whatever you want," he says, reaching inside the cooler.

As the cracker crumbs fly, I turn my attention to the early morning on the open road: the dew-soaked grass, the knee-high prairies, the ever-changing mosaic of hills.

In 1849 one emigrant wrote of an equally wondrous dawn on the road west: "The morning broke clear, beautiful, & refreshing," he remarked. "After a good cup of coffee we were off again with spirits buoyant as air."[1]

Over a century and a half later, my spirit feels similarly.

We've got another 120 miles before Independence, Missouri, the starting line for three historic trails: the California, the Oregon, and the Santa Fe—the combination of which earned the city its title of "Queen City of the Trails." Though just 10 miles east of Kansas City, Independence has been spared the commotion of its big-city neighbor. With a population of 117,000, Independence maintains the conveniences of city life while also retaining its slow-paced charm. The latter of which we observe firsthand as we enter a city half-asleep. Truth be told, Henry and I are still half-asleep ourselves, though our eyes widen upon pulling into the parking lot of the National Frontier Trails Museum, where, parked casually alongside the cars, we spot a mule-drawn wagon.

The man at the reins tips his wide-brimmed hat, then calls to us conspiratorially: "You fellas looking for a ride?"[2]

"Absolutely," Henry says.

Since we have some time before our previously scheduled interview with Oregon-California Trails Association manager Travis Boley, I let Henry's decision stand.

Reaching for my wallet, I pluck out my credit card.

One transaction later the driver offers a dramatic "Yeehaw!" (more for our benefit than the mules') before leading us up West Pacific Avenue, much as tens of thousands of wagons once did. Due to the early hour, Henry and I receive a private tour, huddling close to the driver so as not to miss a word.

"What's your name, son?" the driver calls back to us.

"Henry," he whispers.

"Henry?" the driver repeats. "Well, you gotta say it like you're proud of it! Hen-RY!"

"Hen-RY!" Henry shouts, startling the mules.

7. Ralph and Henry, Independence, Missouri. Courtesy of the author.

"There you go!" he chuckles. "You know, I have a pretty special name myself. You know why?"

"Why?"

"Because I got the only name my dog can pronounce," the driver says. He pauses for the punchline: "Ralph, Ralph, Ralph!"

Henry and I chuckle.

"And up here we got Vietta and Bessie," Ralph continues, introducing us to his mules. "Bessie's named after Bess Truman, President Harry Truman's wife. And Vietta here's named after Bess Truman's maid. Both Bess and Harry grew up right around the corner here."

My face reddens as I realize that I'd been so caught up in Independence's trail history that I'd overlooked its presidential history: home to our thirty-third president.

Though we ride in the president's long shadow, Ralph keeps our attention mostly on the trail.

"I got a question for ya, Henry," Ralph begins. "Which would you rather have, free land or gold?"

"Free land," Henry says without skipping a beat.

"You're a wise man," Ralph says. "Because if you had the gold, somebody would probably shoot ya for it."

Ralph tells us how in May 1845 a New York newspaper man named Horace Greeley (often credited for coining the phrase "Go west, young man") traveled to Independence and, upon his arrival, found something more valuable than gold: a thousand wagons glutting these very streets.

"A thousand?" Henry whispers to me. "Really?"

The image is in stark contrast to the empty streets stretched before us today. Yet between 1841 and 1849 Independence had grown to become the jam-packed jumping-off point Greeley described. Not by accident but for two vitally important reasons. First, Independence's location on the banks of the Missouri River placed the town at the westernmost point for emigrants to outfit and organize for the journey ahead.

Second, since the Santa Fe Trail had been established in Independence as early as the 1820s, trail infrastructure for Oregon- and California-bound travelers was already in place. Throughout the 1840s streams of emigrants regularly disembarked at Independence Landing, made the three-and-a-half-mile hike to the square, and entered into a thriving town that seemed to have sprung from the forest. Supplies were readily available, as was a community of fellow travelers, the majority of whom shared the goal of striking out for the Willamette Valley.

Bouncing in the back of that mule-drawn wagon, I try to conjure the cacophony that once overpowered this town: the steady lowing of oxen, the blasts from the blacksmith shops, and the endless hollering from salesmen anxious to make a buck. I hear braying, barking, gunfire. The wind blowing through trees. The pitter-patter of rain splattering the mud puddles. Children running amok down dirt roads.

For a time Independence inspired as much awe as bewilderment. And for rural folks unaccustomed to the hustle and bustle, the town was a good place to get into trouble. It was only natural that the convergence of thousands of men willing to risk their lives were also

8. Courthouse in Independence, 1855. Engraving by Charles A. Dana. National Archives at College Park, via Wikimedia Commons.

willing to risk their fortunes. Gambling became big business. But the card sharps were only as dangerous as the snake oil salesmen, and there was no shortage of those either.

Yet country folks were hardly the only ones at risk in Independence, and to their advantage, at least they generally knew how to handle a firearm. Out-of-town city folks often didn't.

As one writer put it, "The amount of death and mutilation caused by the sudden arming of men totally unaccustomed to guns was estimated by some to be more than the carnage of all the Indian attacks put together."[3]

Twentieth-century trail scholar and historian Merrill Mattes put an even finer point on it, describing emigrants as "walking arsenals, armed to the teeth with rifles, shotguns, and revolvers." While such weaponry was meant to be used for hunting and defense, as Mattes explains, mostly all the emigrants "managed to do was blast, wound, or annihilate themselves."[4] Since guns had no safeties in those days, all it took was a bump in the road for one to eat one's bullet.

If gambling, snake oil salesmen, and guns weren't enough to put a premature end to the emigrants' journey, they could often count on disease to finish the job. The influx of people and animals made it difficult to prevent feces from entering the water supply, and when it did, lives were inevitably lost. Outbreaks of cholera, dysentery, and typhoid fever were particularly common in frontier towns along the trail, and many emigrants tangled with such scourges while encamped in Independence.

Despite such vices and afflictions, Independence itself remained a place of pristine beauty. In the 1830s a Mormon emigrant noted that the town's nearby prairie lands were "beautiful beyond description." Then, in an effort to prove himself wrong, he described the land anyway: "Meadow peeps o'er meadow, and prairie on prairies rise like the rolling waves on the ocean."[5]

Hints of this landscape still remain, particularly the "rolling waves of the ocean." Yet the waves I'll see later that day are not the same waves the Mormon emigrant saw all those years before. What I'll see are the swales carved into the earth by way of the thousands of wagons that rolled across it during the Oregon Trail's heyday between 1846 and 1869. Though swales are hardly the most dramatic proof of the emigrants' journey, the landscape's depressions are impressive, nonetheless. That the emigrants did the work of glaciers (and at a much faster pace) speaks to their multitudes. Even if we wanted to forget America's westward migration story, the land won't let us. Neither does Ralph.

At the conclusion of our fact-filled tour, Ralph drives Vietta and Bessie back to the National Frontier Trails Museum parking lot.

But before bidding us farewell, Ralph has a few more questions for Henry.[6]

"Those pioneers we've been talking about, they had a dream. Do you know the name of that dream, Henry?"

Since Henry's interest has turned to the mules, I answer on his behalf.

"Manifest destiny?" I try.

"Manifest destiny," Ralph agrees. "Now Henry," he calls, snapping him back to attention, "you must have a dream too. Because without a dream, nobody can help you. Parents cannot help you, teachers cannot help you, the government cannot help you. Not even God almighty can help somebody without a dream. You must find something you're passionate about or called to do and go after it. That is what made our nation great."

Henry nods.

"So?" Ralph asks. "What's your dream? What are you gonna do when you grow up?"

"Toy maker," Henry says.

"A toy manufacturer!" Ralph says. "Well, there you go! Hey, you know what my dream is?"

"What?"

Another pause before the punchline: "To be self-employed and drive a couple of jackasses," he laughs, nodding to his mules.

"You're living the dream, Ralph," I say as we disembark from the wagon.

"You know," he says, tipping his hat, "I really am."

★ ★ ★

It's tough to top a mule-drawn wagon ride, and while the National Frontier Trails Museum is up for the challenge, Henry's anxious to trade in the exhibitions for more adventure. Travis Boley, the Oregon-California Trails Association (OCTA) manager, is happy to assist.[7]

"Let me drive you by a couple of landmarks," he says, leading us out the back of the museum and toward his SUV. "I'll show you a few things kicking around town here."

We buckle up, preparing to cover more ground than the mules could've managed on their best day. At forty-five Travis exudes the so-called pioneer spirit: he's confident, cool, and never met a challenge he didn't want to tangle with. Following stints at the Basketball Hall of Fame and the Pony Express Museum, in 2003 he accepted his current role at the Oregon-California Trails Association, a job that demands a variety of responsibilities: from trail preservation and event planning to research and membership drives. Though his most important job, he explains, is ensuring the Oregon and California Trails' relevancy.

"I think most people have this misconception that the Oregon Trail doesn't exist anymore, at least in terms of it being on the ground," Travis says as we drive north up Liberty Street. "Most people view it as a line on a map." Of course, it's far more than that, which he sets out to prove to us at thirty miles per hour.

We turn right on Lexington Avenue, past Independence Square ("That's where Harry Truman had his first job!"), then farther out toward Sugar Creek one town to the north. Every chance he gets, Travis points out not only the various historic sites that currently line our route but also the sites that once lined it 150 years ago. He sees both past and present with remarkable ease, painting for Henry and me a clear portrait of what once was.

"Let's pull over here," Travis says, parking in a lot high above the Missouri River. "Welcome to the Wayne City Landing."

If it weren't for the signage, I'd have missed it altogether. The thick foliage all but guarantees it. Though after a short stroll through the bramble, from our place atop the bluff, we're rewarded with an unencumbered view of the river below.

"This is sort of a unique spot," Travis says, "because it's one of the few places in America where four trails intersect: Oregon, California, Santa Fe, and Lewis and Clark."

That Lewis and Clark passed this way is news to me. But indeed, their journals describe visiting this very area in late June 1804. Wild apples were picked, according to Clark, not far from this river.

"So how did these trails originally form?" I ask as Henry climbs nearby limestone for a better look at the river.

"Originally it was very organic," Travis explains. "And the credit goes to the American Indians. It was their trails we were following. And I never want people to lose sight of the fact that there were people here before the pioneers."

Yet lose sight of it we do. It is, perhaps, one of the more spectacular omissions of the American consciousness: our ability to remain fixated on the romanticized version of the emigrants' "discovery" of the West while ignoring the fact that their so-called discoveries had actually been discovered, in many cases, centuries before. Yes, white people first laid eyes on Oregon's Columbia River in 1792, though it can hardly be called a discovery given that indigenous people had been calling that river home for the preceding fifteen thousand years.

As emigrants encroached deeper onto their land, indigenous people found themselves and their resources severely threatened. Who were these light-skinned travelers churning up dust in the wake of their wagons? And more important, what did they want?

The emigrants wanted various things—land, gold, freedom, and opportunity, just to name a few. When these self-interested motives no longer seemed sufficient, westward expansion's unofficial public relations campaign sweetened the deal by dragging God into it.

In the summer of 1845 a little-known New York journalist named John O'Sullivan did precisely that. In his essay published in the *Democratic Review*, O'Sullivan informed the nation that it was America's "manifest destiny to overspread and to possess the whole of the continent which Providence has given us."[8]

O'Sullivan's calls for manifest destiny provided the perfect motive for a terrible crime—a land grab that came with both human and cultural consequences. As a result of O'Sullivan's theory, emigrants could rest easier knowing that they weren't usurping more than half of the future continental United States from its indigenous people purely for selfish purposes but, rather, were fulfilling God's wishes.

It was hardly the first time faith had served as a subterfuge.

As scholar Roxanne Dunbar-Ortiz writes, manifest destiny "normalize[d] the successive invasions and occupations of Indigenous nations and Mexico as not being colonialist or imperialist, rather simply ordained progress."[9]

For many emigrants it was a foregone conclusion: not only would their wagon train roll on, but it would do so with God's blessing.

Many would take issue with such a claim—including members of the Sioux nation and the Shoshone and the Dakota and the Snake and the Crow and the Kiowa, among a host of other Native Americans who lost lives, land, and food as the emigrants thundered west. While Hollywood often leads moviegoers to believe that these tribes expressed their anger by way of murderous rampages against the "minding-their-own-business" emigrants, the reality could not be further from the truth. Though some encounters between Native Americans and emigrant ended in bloodshed, more often than not, it was the Native Americans who lost blood.

Between 1840 and 1850 Native Americans were collectively responsible for 362 emigrant deaths, whereas emigrants were responsible for the deaths of 426 Native Americans.[10] One scholar estimates that of the many ways an emigrant might die en route to Oregon and California (illness, injury, accident, or snakebite, among others), a mere 4 percent of deaths were the result of Native American attacks.

Four percent.

Meaning it was more likely that an emigrant would get run over by his own wagon wheel than die at the hands of the people whose world he was upending.

In trying to explain all this to Henry, I tell him that westward expansion and its aftermath is really a story about power—who had it, who didn't, and the price that was paid as a result. But the part I can't explain is how manifest destiny allowed so many nineteenth-century Americans to confuse God with a real estate broker.

As appealing a motive as manifest destiny might've seemed to those emigrants, today it's a reminder of America's darker legacy, one that demands we confront a difficult question: how can we be exceptional and exploitative all at once?

A lifelong student of history, Travis has long considered this question and acknowledges, too, that the romanticized version of westward expansion is best left to the movies rather than the history books. The truth, Travis explains, is that while the majority of Indian-emigrant interactions were peaceful in that era, that wasn't always the case. Moreover, unquestionably, the overall impact of westward travel dramatically diminished the Native American presence and culture in the West.

"What came after the trail era, and as a direct result of the trail era, absolutely reduced their numbers and squeezed them from their traditional homelands to smaller and smaller reservations," Travis says. "That is without dispute and is a simple fact."

In recent years Travis and the Oregon-California Trails Association have worked to tell a more evenhanded version of westward expansion, one that does more than glorify emigrants. To this end OCTA has recently partnered with the Apaches at Fort Bayard in New Mexico, held a recent convention at the Shoshone-Bannock Reservation at Fort Hall, Idaho, and worked alongside the Pawnees in Council Bluffs, Iowa—all in an effort to give voice to perspectives that have historically been silenced.

"American Indians are still here, and their story is important to provide a fuller understanding of this era of history," Travis says. "Trails can help repair old wounds and hurts if we are all willing to work together to tell the most complete story possible by considering all legitimate viewpoints."

If history was simple, perhaps we'd be better at learning from our past mistakes. Yet too often we don't. There's truth in the old platitude: history *does* have a way of repeating itself. But it doesn't have to. Confronting America's past in all its complexities only serves to strengthen its future.

"In some ways 'manifest destiny' is another word for genocide," Travis says as we head back toward his car. "Some people call that revisionist history, and I always say, 'Well, we wouldn't have had to revise it if we'd gotten it correct in the first place.'"

★ ★ ★

Somewhere on the highway between Missouri and Kansas, the landscape grows wilder. The highways give way to backroads, which give way to dirt roads, which give way to virtually no road at all. Henry, who's been questioning my navigation since Wamego, grows sullen in the back seat.

"Almost there," I say cheerily, though the GPS's demand for us to "please make a U-turn" does little to support my claim.

I'd been warned that Alcove Spring—an emigrant hotspot near the Big Blue River—was "off the beaten path." Though in truth this descriptor had made it all the more alluring. Sticking to the well-trod historic sites is one way to experience the American West, but testing the limits of one's four-wheel drive is another.

Just as I begin to curse my newfound adventurous spirit, I spot a small sign directing us toward Alcove Spring.

"There it is," I shout, my enthusiasm so great you'd have thought we'd just arrived at the Willamette Valley.

Waiting for us in the parking lot is Travis's friend Duane Iles, the Oregon-California Trails Association's northeast Kansas chapter president and one of Alcove Spring's main caretakers. Dressed in shorts and a red polo, seven-one-year-old Duane gives us a hearty wave.[11]

"Welcome to Alcove Spring!" he calls. Duane is a walking, talking historic marker—one whose love for these 223 acres in northeastern Kansas knows no bounds. He's proud of the place, as he should be. Not only is it listed in the National Register of Historic Places, but according to Duane, the National Park Service's survey of trails declared Alcove Spring the most significant trail spot in Kansas. Indeed, in terms of trail history Alcove Spring has it all: ruts, swales, even emigrant engravings on the limestone rocks.

Yet it all might've been lost were it not for the efforts of the local chapter of the Rotary Club, which saw fit to buy the land and create the Alcove Spring Historical Trust, of which Duane is a founding member. For the past quarter-century the trust has been committed to a single mission: maintaining the land as it once was. With the exception of light trail work and adding a walking bridge or two, today Alcove Spring looks much as it did when the Donner-Reed party first gazed upon it in May 1846. Though they were just eight or so months removed from their tragic end—trapped, starved, and forced to resort to cannibalism in the Sierra Nevada—such horrors still seemed an impossibility to the optimistic travelers when they rolled their wagons into the pristine landscape now before us.

As Henry and I follow Duane along the sun-dappled trail, he tells us that it's his job to do what he can to maintain its pristineness. "There are no hot dog stands here," he says as we ascend a hill. "And there never will be."

Ten minutes into our hike, our canopy cover vanishes, exposing us once more to the burning Kansas sun. Henry gives me his "are we almost there?" look, which I return with my "how should I know?" shrug.

"The spring's right around this bend here," Duane says, ending the mystery. Henry and I quicken our pace and within moments spot a wide shelving rock on the opposite side of a basin not far from a trickling stream. It's too dry for the water to fall from the shelving rock to the basin below, but it's easy enough to envision. Especially with the help of emigrant Edwin Bryant, who in May 1846 first observed the spring alongside the other members of the Donner-Reed wagon train.

"We found a large spring of water," Bryant wrote, "as cold and pure as if it had just been melted from ice. It gushed from a ledge of rocks, which composes the bank of the stream, and falling some ten feet, its waters are received into a basin." He goes on to note the "beautiful cascade of water" and "shrubbery of the richest verdure" before settling on his final assessment: "Altogether it is one of the most romantic spots I ever saw."[12]

It must have seemed so to the forty-one-year-old newspaper editor from Kentucky who in 1846 left the *Louisville Courier* to write a first-hand account of his westward journey titled *What I Saw in California*. His book details all he saw along the way, including his first glimpse at the spring now stretched before us.

"And the emigrant engravings?" I ask. "They're here too?"

"Right over here," Duane says, leading us down a rocky embankment. "Now watch your step. We haven't really improved it much because we don't want a lot of people coming down."

Keeping our centers of gravity low, Henry and I shuffle toward the water. Upon reaching the bottom, Duane points to the rock that reads, "Alcove Spring." Just a few feet away, we spot a second etching: "JF Reed 26 May 1846."

Prior to researching Alcove Spring, I'd never heard of any "JF Reed," though in fact, his story is quite important to Oregon Trail history.

Who was James F. Reed?

For starters he was a man who defied simple summary. Before becoming the namesake for the latter half of the infamous Donner-Reed party, he was a furniture builder from Springfield, Illinois. Like so many others, in the spring of 1846 forty-six-year-old Reed became afflicted with a bout of Oregon fever and, in an attempt to squelch the scourge, hitched his family's wagon alongside the Donner's—an ill-fated decision, as history would prove. Yet long before the desperate acts of cannibalism that would become synonymous with the Donner name, members of the Donner-Reed party remained downright optimistic for the journey ahead. They had their health, favorable weather, and plenty of supplies. What could possibly go wrong?

Members of the Donner-Reed party were some of the first emigrants to lay eyes on Alcove Spring; in fact, Edwin Bryant is credited with naming it. To make it official, that May a member of the Donner-Reed party etched the land's new name into the top of the rock shelf, and subsequent etchings ensured that the name stuck. Though the Donner-Reed party had planned to pass through, due to the dangerously high level of the Big Blue River, they broke camp, instead, and waited for the water to recede.

While waiting, James Reed's mother-in-law, seventy-year-old Sarah Keyes, grew increasingly ill. Blind and nearing the end of her life, she'd pleaded with her son-in-law to allow her to accompany the family on their journey, and Reed had agreed. Keyes's motive was different than most: she had no interest in gold or land or freedom, merely the hope to reunite with a son who'd struck out for Oregon years earlier. Their reunion was not to be.

In the early morning hours of May 29, 1846, Sarah Keyes took her final breath at the Alcove Spring camp, not far from where we're currently standing. Always the dutiful son-in-law, Reed buried her

9. In search of Sarah Keyes, Alcove Spring, Kansas. Courtesy of the author.

beneath a nearby oak tree. Yet before doing so, he snipped a lock of Grandma Keyes's gray hair as a keepsake for his eight-year-old daughter, Patty. Nine months later—when the Donner party's difficulties were nearing their worst—rescuers found the half-starved girl clutching her grandmother's hair while shivering in the Sierra Nevada.

Yet for the moment Sarah Keyes was the wagon train's only casualty, and given her advanced age and ailing health, her death was hardly unexpected.

At 2:00 p.m. on May 29 all work halted so that every emigrant could pay their respects. Later, when death became an all-too-familiar companion for the wagon train, such formalities were greatly diminished. But in the beginning, when death was rare, all practices and protocols were observed. The emigrants gathered round the grave, sang hymns, and nodded solemnly to the beat of the reverend's benediction. It was a funeral service not unlike what they'd grown accustomed to back home: somber, formal, and full of praise.

Flush with poeticism, Edwin Bryant detailed the funeral in full as well as the stillness that resumed later that evening. "The crescent moon sheds her pale rays over the dim landscape; the whippoorwill is chanting its lamentations in the neighboring grove; the low and mournful hooting of the owl is heard at a far off distance, and altogether the scene, with its adjuncts around us, is one of peace, beauty, and enjoyment."[13]

How wondrous, 172 years later, to stand where the Donner-Reed party once stood. To dip my feet in the spring, place my hands on the rocks, and see and hear and feel what they once did. Though the part we can't re-create is paying our respects to Sarah Keyes. While various trail journals offer clues to her burial spot, today those clues are of little help. The referenced oak is long gone, and though Duane has a general sense of the grave's placement ("I'm guessing it's somewhere between those two trees out there," he tells me at one point), no one knows for sure.

Upon reaching the other side of the road, Duane points toward a slight slope in the grassy landscape. "Now that there," he says, "is a genuine wagon swale."

But since it's our fifth swale of the day, Henry—who has exceeded his swale quota—collapses onto a nearby bench. It's not that he dislikes swales on principle, he's just not sure what he's looking at. I can't blame him. Despite being informed that a swale is a "low place in the land," I barely know myself.

"So . . . that little hump in the grass there?" I ask.

"That's the one," Duane agrees, adding that it's easier to see them at dawn and dusk, when the shadows help them pop from the landscape.

Days later, while driving past a swale in perfect light, I'll see what he's talking about. The way those hints of hollowed land give rise to the bulging grasses, which emerge from the flatness like an optical illusion—there one minute and gone the next.

After a short stroll through the tall grass, Duane suddenly stops mid-step. Placing his hands on his hips, he breathes deep, his eyes scanning the landscape stretched before us.

"There's kind of an aura about the place," Duane says. "Sometimes I just sit by the spring or up on the hill and . . . and I just have a feeling of the history tied to it, of the people who came before."

I feel it too: the whisper of ghost wagons creaking between past and present. It's not a haunting feeling but a comforting one. A reminder that the past lingers everywhere when you know where to look.

As we head back toward the cars, I ask Duane what he hopes Alcove Spring will be like in the future.

"That's easy," he says. "Exactly like it is today."

* * *

After bidding farewell to Duane, Henry and I head north toward the coast of Nebraska. Since the landlocked state has no actual coast, it claims the sandhills as such—a beautiful beach that's only missing water. Though after several long weeks on the trail, the sandhills were a sight nearly as welcome as the ocean: proof for the emigrants that they were headed in the right direction.

According to our GPS, Henry and I are too. Though after logging nearly 400 miles in a single day, we don't much care where we are, as long as we're nearing our destination. The Grand Island Kampground of America in Doniphan, Nebraska, is still 150 miles to the northwest, which seems unfathomable.

"You mean 150 *more* miles?" he asks.

I share his exhaustion; the only difference is that I'm too stubborn to admit it. Though my naive understanding of distances and attention spans has gotten us into this mess, I remain hopeful that my stubbornness might get us out. Yet somewhere between Fairbury and Gilead, even my stubbornness begins to wane. Soon I fall victim to highway hypnosis, losing all sense of the world as I press a lead foot to the gas. I no longer pause to admire the landscape; instead, I focus solely on mileage. The towns blur—Hebron, Geneva, Fairmont—as we pass right on through. Only later, when looking at a map, will I learn their names at all.

Blame it on the heat or the mileage or my pre-exhaustion for the journey that's barely begun. Whatever the reason, in my mind's eye, U.S. 81 is a blank corridor of endless road.

To shake myself from my state, Henry and I return to the question that's plagued us since the previous afternoon: what to name our vehicle? For the emigrants, settling on the appropriate wagon name was essential. Once decided, the name was often displayed on the wagon cover, revealing the creative flourishes of individual families while also serving as an identifying marker within the larger train.

"When such a familiarly marked wagon came into view the overlander felt like welcoming an old friend," one scholar wrote, remarking, too, that there was no shortage of names to choose from: the Tornado Train, Prairie Bird, Albatross, and Red Rover, among countless others. Equally revealing were the more broadly encompassing wagon train mottoes: "Never Say Die," "Oregon, the Whole or None," "Gold or a Grave"—the list goes on.[14]

After twenty-four hours of pondering, Henry and I have yet to find our perfect fit. We'd considered the obvious choices—the Steel Oxen, the Twenty-First Century Wagon, Compass the Jeep Compass—but nothing seemed worthy of the adventure ahead.

While stretching our legs in a church parking lot somewhere in Nebraska, inspiration strikes.

"Bullseye!" Henry calls.

"Huh?"

"That's the name!"

"Why?"

"You know, like the horse from *Toy Story*."

I remind him that horses rarely pulled wagons; that job was generally left to the heartier oxen and mules.

"I didn't pick it because of the animal," Henry says, exasperated. "I picked it because of Bullseye's catchphrase."

"What's his catchphrase?" I ask.

Henry clears his throat, then begins gyrating his hips while swinging his imaginary lasso.

"Ride like the wind, Bullseye!" he cries.

Ride like the wind.

It's the perfect sentiment and one sure to power us through the day's last long stretch of road.

"Well, come on then," I smile, returning to the newly christened Bullseye. "What are we waiting for?"

Leaping into the back seat, Henry buckles up, then hollers at the top of his lungs: "Ride like the wind!"

Pedal to the metal, eyes straight ahead, for the next ninety miles, we do.

10. Henry's illustration of the storm. Courtesy of the author.

3

Weathering the Storm

[A] severe thunder storm . . . took place in the middle of the night. The thunder seemed almost incessant, and the lightning was so brilliant you could read by its flashes. The men chained the oxen so they would not stampede, though they were very restive. Our tents were blown down as were the covers off our prairie schooners and in less than five minutes we were wet as drowned rats . . . You have no idea of the confusion resulting from a storm on the plains, with the oxen bellowing, the children crying and the men shouting, the thunder rolling like a constant salvo of artillery; with everything as light as day from the lightning flashes and the next second as black as the depth of the pit.

—Benjamin Franklin Bonney, 1845

SATURDAY, JUNE 9

WEATHER: RAIN AND SHINE

RATIONS: BUFFALO (BURGERS), TV DINNERS

DONIPHAN NE → KEARNEY NE → OGALLALA NE → SIDNEY NE

At around 2:00 a.m. I wake to the sound of the wind. At first it's nothing more than a gentle breeze rippling against the nylon tent. But soon, those ripples become rattles, and as those rattles increase in speed, I am reminded of what I forgot to do: stake down the tent.

In my defense it wasn't so much that I forgot but that I made a conscious choice not to. In retrospect that probably makes it worse. Nonetheless, the previous night had seemed so perfect—the Grand Island KOA was nothing if not quiet and starlit and still—and so, at the end of our long day on the road, tent stakes had seemed unnecessary.

I mean, it wasn't like we were going to blow away.

Which is precisely the phrase that comes to my mind as the tent poles bend inward.

In my better-late-than-never approach to doing the right thing, I begin to stake down the tent—a task that would've proven infinitely easier were it not the middle of the night. A mallet might've helped, too, but since I'd failed to bring one, I make do with what I've got: my Teva sandals. Upon Velcro-ing them to my feet, I get to work stomping those stakes into the hard earth. Which is about as successful as it sounds. The first stake bends into a horseshoe, while the second nearly punctures my sandal sole. I drop to my knees, then begin driving the stakes by hand, pressing all 140 pounds of me onto those thin shivs as if giving chest compressions to the ground.

Mission accomplished, I glance toward my fellow tent campers, awaiting a bit of applause. I receive none. Not because it isn't warranted but because all my fellow tent campers have apparently vacated the premises.

While I used those vital, pre-storm minutes to batten down the hatches, the others said to hell with the hatches. Rather than put down stakes, they uprooted theirs, collapsing tents and running for shelter in the nearby shower stalls.

Would it have killed someone to tap on my tent and tell me to run for cover? Or to at least kindly suggest that I rethink my half-baked plan?

No matter, I think as the rain bears down. *The important thing is to stay calm.*

A fine bit of advice when one's in a position to do so. But when trapped in a tent with a six-year-old nearly six hundred miles from home, "staying calm" is hardly an option.

"Henry, get your butt up!" I holler. "It's storming!"

"Hmmm?"

"Come on," I say, tugging on his sleeping bag. "Ride like the wind, Bullseye!"

Now more confused than ever, Henry spends the next three minutes trying to unzip himself from his sleeping bag and back into his Ninja Turtles onesie. After freeing himself from the former, he traps himself in the latter, hopping on one foot while searching for a foot hole. Meanwhile, I unthread the tent poles from their nylon holders, collapsing the tent and nearly trapping Henry inside. It occurs to me that we are performing the world's worst Laurel and Hardy routine. And it occurs to me, too, that much of this might have been avoided had I bothered to check the weather radar or stake down the tent or enact any number of cautionary measures. Instead, I'd thrown caution to the wind (along with everything else) and led myself to believe that weather was somehow immutable. That a quiet, starlit night would remain as such, when, in fact, the only guarantee is that it won't.

This isn't my first go-round with inclement weather. In 2011—the day after Meredith and I learned we were pregnant with Henry—we survived an EF4 tornado while hunkered in a bathtub in Tuscaloosa, Alabama. While crouched in that tub alongside our whimpering dog, it became clear to us just how quickly our futures might vanish. We were just one tornado turn away from losing everything. How quickly our joy became terror. We were less afraid of what might happen to us than what might *not* happen. What if we never got to know our future child? What if there was no future child? That we all survived to know each other is a blessing beyond measure. Others were not so lucky. Every storm since, I've kept a close watch on the weather radar. Present storms excluded.

I don't waste time refolding the tent. Instead, as the storm pounds down, I gather it in my arms and toss it into Bullseye's trunk. Henry trails just one step behind me, slipping into a sliver of open seat in the back. Taking my place in the driver's seat, I turn to help Henry assemble his sleeping nest. Upon pushing aside the cooler and the dry bag, I pile both our sleeping bags atop him, swaddling him tight like the old days.

"You okay?" I ask.

He opens his eyes long enough to consider it.

"No," he says.

"No?"

"My hat," he mumbles in the language of half-sleep. "I lost my hat . . ."

Not just any hat but a bright red, big-billed talisman upon which was stitched a creature of indeterminate origin. We'd snagged it at a thrift store a few months back, which gave Henry plenty of time to grow impossibly attached to it. The thought of losing it now, so early in our trip, is more than I can bear.

I prepare myself to brave the storm in search of what's gone missing. But before I even open the car door, I spot a woman's silhouette sprinting toward us. She has a perfect runner's stride: head down, arms pumping, her legs a pair of pistons at full tilt. Backlit by lightning, the woman reaches our passenger side door. Arm raised, she reveals the red hat in her hand.

"Is this yours?" she hollers over the sound of the wind.

I jump out of the driver's seat and run toward her, gripping the soggy hat in my hands.

"Thank you!" I shout.

"No problem!" she shouts back, sopping.

For a moment we stare at each other as if trying to retrace all our decisions—good and bad—that somehow led us to this encounter. We both know we'll never see each other again but also that in this instance we see each other fully. In the thirty seconds we share, I come to know her like a sister. Would you believe me if I told you that I read her entire biography in the contours of her rain-slick face? And that she came to know my own story similarly?

Yet rather than admit such a miracle, we simply retreat to the safety of our shelters.

"Buddy, look what that lady found!" I say, returning to the driver's seat and handing the hat back to him.

"Thanks," he mumbles, plopping it atop his head. He's back to snoring within seconds.

I wish I could manage a few winks, though my adrenaline ensures that I can't. Reaching for my phone in the glove compartment, I find just enough signal to confirm that we are, indeed, in the middle of a severe thunderstorm warning. I could've guessed as much. Returning the phone to the glove compartment, I spend the next half hour listening to the rain clatter atop the car, ten thousand tiny hammers tinging in surround sound. Just ahead of me, beyond a chain-link fence, the campground's pool churns like the ocean.

Maybe Nebraska has a coast after all, I think.

That night I bear witness to every last drop of rain, humbled by how quickly Mother Nature has made short work of us. Any misguided notions I may have had related to gumption or determination quickly fade. I am reminded of who I am: a dad with a plan and little experience to carry it out.

My naïveté fades, and in its place sprouts a new, cruel reality. Though I can't know all that I don't know, I do know that not knowing these things will likely harm us. The heaviness of this realization only adds to my physical fatigue. With the exception of Henry's birth eight and a half months after the tornado, this is the longest night I've ever known. For hours I stare out the rain-soaked windshield, anxiously awaiting the approaching Nebraskan dawn.

The sun rises at 6:02 a.m. Henry stirs soon after.

"How'd you sleep?" I ask as he emerges from his nest.

He sits up, trying to make sense of his surroundings.

"Where . . . am I?" he asks.

"Nebraska," I say.

Moaning, he retreats into his bag.

★ ★ ★

Had I heeded the advice of trail experts, we might've avoided the storm altogether.

"A storm can come up in a hurry and travel at thirty-five miles per hour," one wrote, "and should the traveler be short of his midpoint with a cloud between him and his destination, he is well advised to turn around and get the hell out of there."[1]

Wise words which, next time around, I'll take under advisement.

But whether you spot them or not, there's no stopping a prairie storm. They have long been a nuisance for travelers, one scholar describing them as "dangerous as well as uncomfortable." The rain fell "all at once like a solid thing," the passage continues, with hail ranging "from the size of a hen's egg to that of a lemon or peach."[2]

Yet what surprises me most of the emigrants' descriptions of these storms is the ferocity with which they struck.

Nineteenth-century emigrant Ezra Meeker—who regularly traversed the Oregon Trail to bring attention to the need to preserve it—endured his fair share of inclement weather throughout his many trips. "Storms would wet the skin in less time than it takes to write this sentence," he reported. "The cattle traveled so fast it was difficult to keep up with them . . . there was not a dried thread left on me in an incredibly short time." Meeker described his boots filling with water and how the rain poured through his hat like a "sieve."[3]

In 1845, a fellow emigrant described a storm similarly, noting lightning "so brilliant you could read by its flashes." In five minutes the winds had not only downed their wagon train's tents but also stripped the covers straight from their wagons. "We were wet as drowned rats," the emigrant lamented. Though their physical discomfort was only one aspect of their suffering. "You have no idea of the confusion resulting," the emigrant continued, describing the lowing oxen, the weeping children, the hollering men, and the thunder "rolling like a constant salvo of artillery."[4]

Henry and I had been spared all of that—no lows, no weeping, and no hollering aside from my own.

So we got a little wet and lost a little sleep.

It was a small price to pay for a lesson.

★ ★ ★

Since the U.S. Army could hardly protect emigrants from inclement weather, they turned their attention to the so-called Native American threat instead. Though the majority of interactions between emigrants and Native Americans remained positive throughout the 1840s, the occasional skirmish was enough to persuade the government to take action: most notably, by constructing a series of forts to support the emigrants' journey. In 1848 the U.S. Army founded Fort Kearny in south-central Nebraska. While the fort's placement along the trail

11. Fort Kearny blacksmith shop. Courtesy of the author.

may have deterred attacks from the Cheyenne, Sioux, and other regional tribes, its more practical purpose was as a supply post. And a much needed one given its location 317 miles from the outfitting operations back in Independence.

In addition to resupplying the emigrants, Fort Kearny's blacksmith shop further ensured the fort's popularity. Forges and anvils were rare on the plains, and given the importance of keeping one's beasts of burden properly shod, the wise emigrant knew to make good use of the facility. Though less vital to their journey's success, the fort's post office served as another enticement for emigrants to pull to the wayside. After traveling hundreds of miles in relative isolation, emigrants were desperate for some scrap of news related to the well-being of loved ones back home or further along. Of course, receiving letters was but half of the joy of the post office; for new arrivals to Fort Kearny, equally exciting was the opportunity to send letters home.

Given its roles as a supply post, a blacksmith shop, and a post office, it's hard to overstate the importance of Fort Kearny. As one historian put it, "Just as in ancient times all roads led to Rome, so on the frontier of the Great American Desert all roads led to Fort Kearny on the Platte."[5] Indeed, the fort's placement on the Platte River did much to ensure its longevity. By placing it on the Platte—and directly upon the trail—emigrants had even more reasons to stop. There was grass for grazing, water to drink, and plenty of good company.

Much like Fort Kearny, the Platte River, too, connected everything. The only difference: humankind made one, while nature made the other. Not only did the Platte provide an endless water supply for humans and animals alike, but for one thousand miles between Nebraska and Wyoming, its northern fork served as the emigrants' most reliable guide.

The Platte River was the needle that stitched our country whole, weaving between mountains and deserts and giving emigrants a river along whose shores they built their road. Today that road is known as the Great Platte River Road—an eight-hundred-mile corridor that traces a good chunk of the river. Historians have referred to it as "the superhighway of westward expansion," which indeed captures the regularity with which it was traveled.[6]

A little before 9:00 a.m., Henry and I strike out on that super-highway ourselves, making the forty-five-mile drive between our campsite in Doniphan and our first stop of the day, Fort Kearny State Historical Park.

Since we're early for our 10:00 a.m. appointment with park super-intendent Gene Hunt, Henry and I indulge in a little parking lot breakfast. I open the cooler to snag us a couple of yogurts, though upon peeling their foil lids, I'm overcome with the stomach-churning smell of spoiled dairy.

Probably should have sprung for that fresh bag of ice back at the KOA, I think.

"What's wrong?" Henry asks.

"Nothing," I'm quick to answer. "Hey, how do you feel about peaches, granola, and fruit snacks for breakfast?"

"I feel good about that."

I walk the cooler toward the nearest trash can, lightening our load by a dozen or so yogurts.

"Um . . . Dad?"

12. Breakfast in the Fort Kearny parking lot, Kearney, Nebraska. Courtesy of the author.

"Yeah?"

"Why are you throwing away all our yogurt?"

"You think the emigrants had yogurt?"

"Well . . . no," he says, weighing his words carefully. "But they didn't have fruit snacks either."

I sigh.

"Dad?"

"Yeah?"

"Did the yogurt go bad?"

"That's a very real possibility."

Pause.

"You probably should have bought that bag of ice back at the—"

"Yeah, yeah, yeah . . ."

I grab our breakfast's à la carte items, then join Henry on the slow walk toward the picnic table facing a cornfield. We sit atop it, basking in the early-morning glow.

Though our day has just begun, I'm already exhausted.

"Hey bud?" I yawn.

"Yeah, Dad?" he asks.

"You wouldn't happen to have a cup of coffee on ya?"

He turns his pockets inside out.

"Sorry," he says. "Not today."

* * *

Given Fort Kearny's many luxuries, it was not uncommon for emigrants to spend a few days encamped at the fort. Unfortunately, our schedule doesn't allow for it. But since Henry and I have no need for an anvil, a post office, or supplies (well, maybe yogurt), we're hopeful our two-hour allotment will suffice.

Following our examination of the cannon in the sod-roofed blacksmith shop, Henry and I return to the fort's exterior, where we're met by a man loping toward us.

"You must be the fellas from Wisconsin," says park superintendent Gene Hunt. "Let me give you the tour."[7]

It's the same tour he's been giving since arriving at the fort in 1972. Following a decade as the park's assistant superintendent, Gene was promoted to his current position, a role that allows him to blend his love for historic preservation alongside maintenance duties. Both of which are vital in allowing visitors to get a sense of the place more than a century and a half after its heyday.

While Gene offers an overview of the fort's history, Henry—perhaps fearful that we'll soon turn to the subject of swales—darts toward a downed cottonwood tree near the parade grounds at the edge of the square.

"Is it okay for him to be climbing around on that old tree?" I ask.

"Oh sure," Gene says. "In fact, that's the last original cottonwood tree that Lt. Daniel P. Woodbury planted shortly after the fort's founding."

"Woodbury who?" I ask.

"Lt. Daniel P. Woodbury," Gene repeats.

West Point class of 1836, I'll later learn, and the engineer responsible for overseeing the construction of both Fort Kearny (where we stand today) and Fort Laramie (where we'll be standing in a few days). As Fort Kearny neared completion, Woodbury commemorated the occasion by planting dozens of cottonwood trees, thirteen of which remained as of 1972, though they continued to fall in the decades that followed. According to Gene, the last of Woodbury's cottonwoods—the one Henry's climbing up now—held firm until a storm struck in the spring of 1997. Aside from the land itself, that tree served as the last witness to the fort's long history—a living link to connect the past with the present.

We watch from fifty yards out as Henry slips into a large crevice near the tree's base, dropping into a hollowed cavern in its interior and disappearing from view. I try to imagine what the fort might've looked like when all those cottonwoods stood. Back when the traffic jam of wagons creaked into Fort Kearny from late May through early July. I imagine the tens of thousands of anxious emigrants awaiting their turn at the anvil. And the long line of folks streaming forth from the post office. But despite my best efforts, my imagination falls short.

Much like our time at Alcove Spring, this place, too, feels like a ghost town. The blacksmith hammers have been silent for well over a century, and the post office hasn't delivered a letter in years. But even in its mostly silent state, echoes of the fort's liveliness still remain. The soldier rising from his bed for morning reveille. The buffalo herd just beyond rifle's range.

What must it have been like to spend a day here? I wonder.

The journals and diaries can only ever tell us so much. And though I've read them and now know of a few of the fort's highlights (the day Kit Carson visited, for example), what I'll never understand is the impact of these experiences on the emigrants themselves. There's no shortage of day-to-day dispatches, but what I want to know most—and the question I'll ask everyone I meet—is what modern Americans stand to learn from our emigrant predecessors.

Gene pauses when I put the question to him.

"Well," he begins, "I'd say that one of the things we need to learn today is how to slow down."

"Just . . . slow down generally?" I ask.

He nods.

"You see, if a wagon train didn't have a good boss, they'd try to push the train seven days a week, which would wear out the livestock in no time. But the good bosses," he continues, "they knew to take a day of rest." He pauses, peering at the flag snapping in the wind just ahead of us. "Today we're very fast-paced," he continues, "and we're always buying more stuff than we need. And then we're just throwing that stuff out anyway. Probably one of the things our society needs to say is, 'Let's just be a little more focused on where we're going and how we're going to get there. And let's acknowledge, too, that it'll take some time.'"

His advice hits close to home. We're barely two days into our trip, and already I fear I've pushed us much too hard. And to what end? So that we could arrive at our next destination at the arbitrary time I'd set for us? How quickly I'd dispensed with that dump truck's advice to "Make every mile a memory."

I take Gene's advice to heart. But buried within it, I hear another sentiment, one related to the twenty-first-century approach to materialism. By which I mean our insatiable desire to own everything. Perhaps *materialism* is the wrong word for the emigrants' problems with their possessions. For them it was more of a packing issue. How could a family ever manage to compress all their earthly belongings into forty-eight square feet of wagon? Some emigrants made the mistake of trying to make use of all of those feet while forgetting the well-being of the animals tasked to do the pulling. In those instances the oxen generally took matters into their own hooves. Deciding they'd had quite enough of the ill-conceived charade, they expressed their dissatisfaction in one of two ways: by refusing to pull or dying.

Mules, true to their nature, responded with equal stubbornness.

On July 3, 1849, while attempting to cross the Green River, one mule chose the more expedient method of ending his service. According to an emigrant witness, the mule "cooly and deliberately committed suicide. It did not attempt to swim, but allowed its head to go under immediately on its going in the water & neither turned [to] come out, or struggled to save himself, [in] the least."[8]

In response to such dramatic protests, the emigrants began one of America's favorite pastimes: indiscriminately hurling garbage to the side of the road. They did so out of necessity. "Everything taken at the outset was deemed indispensable," one historian wrote. "The definition of indispensability was rapidly revised in the interest of survival and priorities established on the scales of size, weight, and immediate usefulness."[9]

Farewell to the barrels and the basins and the anvils. To the water-colors and the furniture too. If it couldn't preserve life, it was a risk to life and an indulgence they could no longer afford.

For my own part, in the days leading up to our trip I'd begrudgingly let go of my own "less practical" baggage, most gut-wrenchingly my books. I replaced my doorstoppers with more essential and modestly sized volumes: Francis Parkman's *The Oregon Trail* and Julie Fanselow's *Traveling the Oregon Trail*. Parkman's 1849 account earned its spot by providing an historical (albeit morally questionable by today's standards) depiction of his travels west, while Fanselow's book, published 143 years after Parkman's, offered detailed information for today's travelers. Both would prove vital to the journey ahead in vastly different ways.

Our trip's music selection underwent an equally rigorous test, though after many extensive conversations, Henry and I settled upon a few dozen CDs that passed my criteria of (a) being "road trip appropriate"—read: worthy of serving as the soundtrack for the greatest trip of our lives—and (b) being unlikely to drive me insane.

"Which means no *Mickey Mouse Clubhouse*," I'd said, removing it from the CD case.

"But Dad—"

"It's a mental health issue for me."

"But—"

"Look, I compromised on *The Lion King* soundtrack, but I've got to draw the line somewhere."

He'd chewed it over, then offered his rebuttal.

"Well why do you get to bring two copies of *James Taylor's Greatest Hits*?" he asked.

"James Taylor is an American treasure," I'd said. "We always pack a spare."

Much as it was for the emigrants, our "less-is-more" approach to packing was ultimately the right choice. Not only for reasons of physical space but mental space as well. Gene's emigrant-inspired advice to slow down and live simply reinforced our packing philosophy, but it also applied to life more generally: slow down, want not, breathe deep. Had Gene or the emigrants had a probiotic cleanse to add to this philosophy, they'd have had a self-help brand ready for market.

Of all the wisdom I'd gained during my short stint at Fort Kearny, it's the slowing down part that matters most. I know what I need to do—ease off the accelerator both on this trip and beyond.

For the next 150 miles to Ogallala, I stay in the right lane. It's not much, but it's a start.

"Dad," Henry says as we drive away from the fort.

"Yeah, bud?"

"Can we listen to music?"

"What do you want?" I ask.

"Anything," he says, "but James Taylor."

★ ★ ★

Long before it served as a memorable setting for Larry McMurtry's *Lonesome Dove*, Ogallala, Nebraska—the state's self-proclaimed "Cowboy Capital"—was the last stop on the Great Western Cattle Trail. At the cattle trail's peak between 1875 and 1885, cowboys drove countless herds from southern Texas to the frontier town of Ogallala, where the longhorns were sold, fattened, and shipped on the Union Pacific railroad, bringing beef throughout the region and beyond. Unquestionably, we have the cattle drive to thank for the formation of Ogallala. But also, we have the cattle drive to blame.

The town wasn't always a lawless, blood-soaked hotbed for violence, though there was a stint in the 1870s when this depiction teetered a little too close to the truth. By 1875 Ogallala consisted of cowboys, cattle, and thriving saloons, which created the ideal conditions for

13. Greetings from Front Street, Ogallala, Nebraska. Courtesy of the author.

hypermasculinity to run amok.[10] To pass the time between drives, cowboys could curl up with a good book or stir up trouble. I'll leave it to the reader to decide which of the two was more popular.

If they weren't shooting each other, they were stealing each other's cattle. Or enjoying a brawl. Or gambling away freshly earned money. But since "Welcome to Ogallala: Home of Murder, Theft, and Gambling" didn't sit well with the local visitor's bureau, the town rebranded to become the Cowboy Capital. It is, in all respects, a market-savvy alternative—one that retains a whiff of those rough-and-tumble days while steering clear of the specifics.

Today the town's cowboy legacy remains, as evidenced by the forty-foot cowboy-shaped signage that greets us as we pull into town.

"Guess we're in the right place," I say, steering toward Front Street—a tourist-friendly stretch of nineteenth-century-looking store-fronts. Though it lacks tumbleweed, in all other ways Front Street is precisely what I'd dreamed it might be: a dust-caked wonderland of era-specific wagons, wooden fences, and a string of shops identi-fied (from left to right) as the Livery Barn Café, the Crystal Palace Saloon, the Undertaker, the Tonsorial Palace, and of course, the Jail.

We park Bullseye, then practice our cowboy swagger all the way to the swinging doors of the Crystal Palace Saloon. As we approach, my eyes fall to the woman we're here to meet, Mary Cone. In the weeks preceding our trip, I'd reached out to Mary on the advice of the Ogallala Chamber of Commerce, which had assured me that Mary—a local rancher and National Pony Express Association member—would have plenty to share about the city's history.

"You must be B.J.," Mary says, walking over to greet me. "And you," she continues, "you must be Henry!"[11]

Henry, who for a few of our interviews has fallen into the role of third wheel, revels in his newfound attention. Though he's hot, tired, and more than a little perturbed by my less-than-truthful accounts of mileage between destinations, his troubles fade as Mary peppers him with questions about our trip.

"What's your favorite part? What have you seen?"

Henry takes full advantage of his rapt audience. He recounts the high points (our mule-drawn wagon ride with Ralph, the search for Sarah Keyes's grave, the cannon at Fort Kearny) as well as the low points (most of which involve swales and storms).

Mary smiles, then turns to give me the once-over.

"You're younger than I expected," she says.

"Well, I won't look it after this trip," I assure her.

We're greeted by the host, who seats us at a circular table in a horse stall in the corner of the saloon. The restaurant is relatively empty, though what it lacks in clientele it makes up for with kitsch: taxidermy, black-and-white photos, and grandiose, old-timey chandeliers hanging from the rafters.

"Vance and Karen have agreed to join us," Mary says as she distributes the menus. "They're the real scholars of the batch." She's referring to Vance and Karen Nelson, a pair of longtime Nebraskans who, after careers in history curation and education, respectively, retired and moved to Ogallala in 2011. Their knowledge of the Oregon Trail—and all things Nebraska—will help me fill in more than a few historical holes.

They enter moments later, broad smiles on their faces as they welcome us to town.[12] Vance pulls up the chair alongside me, while Karen, a retired schoolteacher, immediately engages Henry with various questions, many of which he'd just answered for Mary. Though Henry's so tickled by his newly formed entourage that he's more than happy to repeat himself. He draws out his answers as long as he can, and I don't blame him. After two long days in a car with me, the dam bursts, and the words come flooding out.

"And just look at his curly hair," Mary raves. "Don't you just love his hair?"

"It's from my dad," Henry tells them, and the women nod approvingly.

"My brother's got hair like that," Vance says, reaching into his wallet. He hands both Henry and me his business card, which identifies him as a public historian. For decades he served, too, as the curator for Fort Robinson, a former U.S. Army fort in western Nebraska. If asked, Vance would gladly relay the fort's complete and unabridged history—from its role in the Sioux Wars to the death of Crazy Horse to the Cheyenne Outbreak of 1879, among various other historic events that occurred until the fort's closing in 1948.

But before we get to all that history, we turn our attention to the menus. Henry and I embrace a "when in Rome" philosophy, ordering the thickest, juiciest buffalo burgers Ogallala has to offer. And then, in an act that seems more for shock value than sustenance, Henry drags a finger down the menu and adds, "You know, I think I'll order a side salad too."

"Um . . . okay," the waiter says. "One side salad for the young man."

"With ranch dressing," Henry adds, handing the waiter the menu. "Thank you."

The ordering of the side salad (which will go down in family lore as "The Side Salad Incident of Ogallala"), coupled with Henry's insistence on a lemon wedge in his ice water, prompts me to wonder if these aren't signs of scurvy. As I reflect on the past thirty-six hours' worth of meals, it occurs to me that the closest we've come to a vegetable was the pickle on my McDonald's burgers two days earlier. As for fruit, well, fruit snacks are a fruit.

As we chat about the town and its history, one fact soon becomes clear: Ogallala is a beloved place, especially for those seated in the stall alongside me.

"What makes us so special," Mary explains, "is that we've got a whole lot of trails tying together here. We've got the Oregon Trail and the Pony Express Trail just to the south and the Mormon Trail just to the north. And then there's the Great Western Cattle Trail coming up from the south. And Ogallala is just kind of the center of it all."

Admittedly, prior to my visit I'd never pegged Ogallala as the center of much of anything. In fact, the only reason I'd included it on the itinerary was because it seemed like a good halfway point between Fort Kearny and our day's destination of Bridgeport, Nebraska. Imagine my surprise upon learning of all the Cowboy Capital had to offer—trail history, cattle herd history, and as Henry will later attest to, the finest side salad in Nebraska.

For the next hour the five of us enjoy our leisurely lunch. Vance regales us with tales of childhood trips to Fort Laramie and Fort Kearny as well as stories about his father, a building contractor who created a cement marker for Chimney Rock, one of the trail's geological gems, which we'll visit the following day.

Karen, meanwhile, shares stories of her time teaching at a school primarily serving Dakota people in Fort Totten, North Dakota.

"One thing I always remember," Karen says, "is how much those students used to love playing the *Oregon Trail* computer game."

"Really?" I ask, nearly choking on my buffalo burger. "Your Native American students were okay with that game's depiction of Native Americans?"

"Oh sure," Karen says. "They thought it was funny."

It wasn't the reaction I'd expected.

The computer game that inspired a generation to virtually hunt buffalo, ford rivers, and make their way to Oregon has in recent years been criticized for its earlier version's stereotypical depictions of Native people. Embarrassingly, such depictions didn't even register to the seven-year-old me; I was naive, full of privilege, and so utterly hypnotized by my first experience with a computer that I didn't raise so much as an eyebrow at the game's one-sided view of history.

The story of the game's development is nearly as compelling as the game itself. In 1971 Don Rawitsch, Bill Heinemann, and Paul Dillenberger—three student teachers from Minnesota's Carleton College—began dreaming up a unique way to teach Rawitsch's students about westward migration. The trio eventually settled on creating a computer game, a version of which was released by the Minnesota Education Computing Consortium (MECC) a few years later. MECC went on to distribute some sixty-five million copies, making it a staple in schools and libraries throughout the country. Though the game has provided countless hours of fun, its most lasting contribution is what it's done to introduce late-twentieth-century students to Oregon Trail history—or some version of it. No book or film has done half so much to share this story with that audience. It's easy to write the game off as entertainment (or "edutainment," as some have called it), though the fact remains that today, nearly half a century after the game's creation, we're still warning one another not to "die of dysentery"—one of the game's most memorable (and meme-able) lines.

But as a teaching tool, the game falls short. In a recent interview with cocreator Don Rawitsch, he shares with me his one regret: not dedicating more time to researching the full impact of westward movement on Native Americans.[13]

"The diaries I read did mention settlers receiving help from these people, and such events were built into the game's original version," Don says. "But the impact was far more negative to Native Americans."

Yet according to Karen Nelson, in addition to enjoying the challenge of the game, her students also reveled in the opportunity to poke fun at the game's inaccuracies related to their ancestors. Karen, who worked with this population of students for years, had often witnessed this particular brand of humor. Did those students feel it was better to laugh it off rather than give power to such depictions?

What, I wonder, *would Karen's students think if they embarked upon another round of that pixelated journey today? And what might I think if I returned to the game's earlier, less culturally sensitive version?*

Henry takes one last noisy sip of ice water as our *Oregon Trail* computer game conversation winds down. After issuing a deep sigh, he laments, "You know, I died in that game too."

Before he can leverage his virtual death for some dessert, the waiter does the hard work for him.

"Can I offer the table some complimentary cake?"

"Yes," Henry says. "You may."

"Sure you don't want another salad?" I whisper.

He tells me where I can stuff my salad.

★ ★ ★

Following our afternoon of buffalo burgers and sun-scorched land-scapes, Henry and I find ourselves fading fast. We've already logged two hundred miles, but in order to make Bridgeport by nightfall, we still have another ninety to go. Which would've seemed more manageable were it not for my storm-filled, sleepless night.

Somewhere near the town of Chappell, Lynyrd Skynyrd's "Sweet Home Alabama" bursts on the radio. Figuring it's our best shot at a second wind, I crank it loud and lower the windows. The hot wind stirs Henry from his self-induced stupor, and he peers up from his composition book to catch my eyes glancing at him in the rearview.

"Sweeeeeetttt hoooooome Alabama!" I caterwaul. "Where the skies are so blue . . ."

My middle-aged white guy head bob enters full throttle, which I accompany with my off-key steering wheel thumps.

Henry, who assumes these are seizure symptoms, asks if I require medical attention.

"Come on!" I cry. "Sing along!"

"I don't know the words."

"Then . . . head bob along!"

For four minutes and forty-five seconds we do just that, bobbing our heads and belting out the chorus and muddling our way through the rest. Though we're short on musical talent, we've got plenty of enthusiasm, which we demonstrate by thrusting our hands out the windows as if trying to snag the wind. Midway through, Henry takes a cue he learned from our dog and peeks the top of his head out the window. The wind whips through his curls, blasting him with its warmth.

It's the happiest I've seen him all day, which means it's the happiest I've been all day too.

But not even Lynyrd Skynyrd can maintain the magic forever, and much of it fades by song's end. I turn down the volume, roll up the windows, and we return to our road-weary selves. Glancing at the GPS, I see that we've still got a butt-numbing sixty miles ahead of us.

"How much longer?" Henry asks.

"Oh, just a little ways."

He scoffs. By now he knows a lie when he hears one.

But what am I to do? I can't shorten the distance any easier than I can steer us clear of a storm. Or redirect a river. Or move a mountain range. As recent events have confirmed, I can't even keep yogurt from spoiling, let alone alter the landscape.

Half an hour later, when we pull over for gas in Sidney, our destination of Bridgeport seems like an impossibility. The GPS says forty more miles, but following a storm-soaked night and a scorching day, that distance seems just shy of Mars.

"How about you get out and stretch your legs?" I suggest as I insert the nozzle into the tank. Henry doesn't need to be told twice. He marches around the car, engaging in an impromptu calisthenics routine—hamstring stretches, calf stretches, and neck rolls to offset the head bobbing.

Directly to my left and just overhead, I spot a Days Inn sign. On its marquee, a single, glorious word: *Pool.*

Suddenly I'm faced with a predicament: do I stick with the plan and get us to Bridgeport? Or do we nix the plan and book ourselves a pool-adjacent room?

Upon reflecting on Gene Hunt's emigrant-inspired lesson on resting one's oxen, the decision becomes easier.

It's not about shortening the distance, I realize, it's about altering our destination. And that much I can manage.

"Hey buddy," I say, interrupting him mid–waist bend, "what do you say we call it a day?"

He straightens his body, eyeing me skeptically.

"What do you mean?"

I point to the marquee.

"Pooooo-ooool?" he reads.

I nod.

He doesn't openly weep at our good fortune. But almost.

★ ★ ★

A year later, when I think back on this day, I won't remember much about the cottonwood trees at Fort Kearny or the buffalo burgers in Ogallala. What I'll remember is a motel pool in some place called Sidney, Nebraska. And how the dust drifted from our bodies amid our belly flops. I'll remember the smell of chlorine, the hot Nebraskan air, and how, when we looked beyond the pool's rim, we could just make out the gas station where we'd settled upon our best decision yet. That afternoon we cannonballed ourselves to smithereens. It was all the rejuvenation we required.

That night, shortly before sundown, Henry and I embark upon one last hike, venturing a full tenth of a mile from the motel to the Walmart across the parking lot. We enter through the automatic doors, paying close attention to the markings of civilization: air-conditioning, donuts, and rotisserie chickens sizzling beneath warming lamps.

Since we don't have anything better to do, we dedicate half an hour to the frozen food aisle, where we painstakingly try to determine what we'll eat for dinner that night: Kid Cuisine or Stouffer's lasagna.

Upon making our selections (one of each), we begin our stroll back toward the motel. The parking lot that separates us from our destination is all heat and concrete, tufts of grass poking through wherever they can. Near the back of the lot, a half dozen truckers have made themselves a makeshift home. One trucker and his partner step from their cab, and a dog hops out behind them. They've had a long day on the road, no doubt, as have we. We nod in solidarity.

As we reach the motel door, I peer back from where we've come. Compared to the wondrous landscapes that have spoiled us throughout the day, the parking lot leaves much to be desired.

"It sure is a beautiful view," I say sarcastically.

"You know," Henry says, missing my snark, "it really is."

How desperately I wish I could still see the world as he does. And how embarrassed I am that I can't.

Reentering our room, we microwave our dinners, split a blackberry juice for dessert, then kick back for an evening of cartoons.

As dusk descends, I slip into the parking lot to retrieve our toiletry bag from Bullseye's trunk. En route I notice the pink sun sinking before my eyes. Standing beside a garbage can, I watch it coat the lot with color.

"You know, you missed a good sunset out there," I say, returning to the room.

If he hears me, he makes no indication.

My first instinct is to click off the TV and march him outside to enjoy the sunset.

But I don't. After all, he saw the beauty in this place *before* the sunset.

Instead, I take my spot alongside him and close my eyes.

And make this mile a memory too.

14. Henry's illustration of our visit to Chimney Rock. Courtesy of the author.

4

Faith and Consequences

Traveled all day in sight of the Chimney . . . Above this spar of hard earth or rock there appeared one of the grandest scenes I ever beheld.

—Asahel Munger, 1839

SUNDAY, JUNE 10

WEATHER: HOT

RATIONS: SARSAPARILLA

SIDNEY NE → BAYARD NE → GERING NE → FORT LARAMIE WY → DOUGLAS WY

It was called many things: the teepee, the smokestack, the lightning rod, the chimneyby, and to the Lakota people, elk penis. But to most it's known simply as Chimney Rock, western Nebraska's very own spire in the sky. As Oregon Trail geological landmarks go, it's unrivaled. Scotts Bluff and Independence Rock—while impressive in their own right—fail to carry the same psychological weight as their more famous (and phallic) geological cousin.

Shortly after breakfast, Henry and I pull into the parking lot to the Chimney Rock National Historic Site. This is our climactic moment after misidentifying the famous rock at least half a dozen times. Which is embarrassing to admit given that there are no similar formations between Sidney and Bayard.

Yet once we pull into the clearly marked lot, there's no mistaking it.

"Wow!" Henry marvels. "This sure beats a swale!"

I imagine the emigrants felt similarly. They'd long dreamed of laying eyes on the natural wonder, not only for what it was but for what it represented: the geological marker that assured the

Oregon-bound emigrants that they were a third of the way there. The rock was a beacon of hope, a landlocked lighthouse, hallowed ground reaching toward the heavens. Even the most lackluster journal-keeping emigrants made note of it, though their descriptions are as varied as the rock's nicknames. In 1845 Joel Palmer wrote that Chimney Rock possessed "the unpoetical appearance of a hay stack with a pole running far above its top."[1] The same year Lt. Col. Phillip St. George Cooke compared the "lofty white Chimney Rock" to "the pharos of a prairie sea."[2] Capt. Benjamin Bonneville called it "among the curiosities of the country," while Rufus B. Sage referred to it as a "wonderful display of the eccentricity of Nature."[3]

It is all of these things and more. And since no self-respecting emigrant could let such a novelty go unchallenged, they did what came naturally: used it for target practice. One hopefully apocryphal story describes a group of soldiers firing a cannon toward the spire and taking off a good four feet. Who can know for sure? What we do know is that between 1885 and the late 1990s, Chimney Rock shrunk by eighteen feet.[4] Erosion deserves most of the blame, along with a 1992 lightning strike.

When Chimney Rock wasn't being fired upon, it was employed for solo climbing expeditions. Many a foolhardy amateur attempted to reach its peak, though none were successful. The spire was simply too steep, the sandstone forever crumbling in their hands. In 1849 Lucius Fairchild claimed to have "climbed up as far as anybody" and noted the "splendid" view of the burgeoning country below.[5] One hundred and sixty-nine years later, the landscape remains as splendid as ever.

Upon entering the visitor center, we're greeted by curator Loren Pospisil. The bespectacled fifty-four-year-old in khakis and white button-up offers me his hand.[6]

"Why don't we find some seats over here," he suggests, leading us toward a pair of rocking chairs near a scenic picture window.

"So," I begin, "tell me about Chimney Rock."

It's like asking an astronomer to talk about space.

15. Hair imitates geography at Chimney Rock, Bayard, Nebraska. Courtesy of the author.

Thankfully, Loren handles my question with good cheer, telling me that what makes Chimney Rock unique is that it's not altogether unique. In fact, thirty states have a geological feature with the very same name. For Loren, who has served as the historic site's superintendent for twenty-four years, the rock isn't half as important as the stories of the hundreds of thousands of people who passed by it. Many of whom were average, run-of-the-mill, middle-class people in search of better lives.

"Rich people, by and large, didn't go on the trail because they had the things they needed," Loren explains. "And poor people didn't go because they couldn't afford the oxen and wagon. So it was mostly middle-class farmers on the trail."

There are plenty of exceptions, though the general idea of westward travel as a middle-class endeavor had never occurred to me. They had too little to be content and too much not to consider it. Meaning they were perfectly susceptible to Oregon fever.

Of course, middle-class emigrants were not alone in making use of the Great Platte River Road. Soon telegraph wire followed the road as well, then the Pony Express, then the transcontinental railroad, then the Lincoln Highway, then the transcontinental airmail route, and finally, fiber optic telephone lines. That one narrow swath of land could prove so vital to America's growth seems astonishing, but perhaps it shouldn't. As Loren explains, the emigrants used this route for the same reason everyone else would both before and after—it was the shortest, flattest, and easiest path between two points.

"History never really ends," Loren says, "it just changes technologies."

Throughout our conversation I keep an eye on Henry, who, at a nearby drawing station, busies himself with my own preferred technology: paper and pen. He's immersed in his drawing, stealing glances at Chimney Rock outside the window and committing what he sees to the paper. Pegged ahead of him on the wall are hundreds of Chimney Rock sketches, the handiwork of a school years' worth of student-age visitors. By the looks of things, Henry's excited to offer his own contribution.

I catch Henry's eye, and when he notices me noticing him, a devious smile creeps across his face.

"Excuse me for a moment," I say to Loren, rising and making my way to the drawing station.

"How you doing, bud?"

"Oh, fine."

"What ya drawing?"

"Nothing," he says, followed by a ham-handed attempt to hide his sketch behind his back.

"Hand it over," I say.

"Hand what over?"

I confiscate the paper, holding it at arm's length to examine the evidence.

"So what do we got here?"

"It's Chimney Rock."

"And who's this guy heroically scaling his way to the top?"

"That's me."

"And who's this schmuck flailing all the way down?"

"That's you."

Looking closer at his sketch, I realize I needn't have asked at all. Scrawled beside his own stick figure is the word *Me*, while alongside his grim-faced stick figure father he's written *BJ Hollars*.

"You were really going to peg this up there with the other drawings?" I ask. "You were going to let the world see your dad—who you *clearly identified*—falling off the side of Chimney Rock?"

"Of course!" he grins.

"Not on my watch," I say. "This sketch is never finding its way to that pegboard."

"But Dad," he whines, "didn't I do a good job?"

"Well, sure," I say, giving it a second look, "though you could've been a little more generous with my biceps."

"Then why are you taking it?" he asks.

"Because," I say, "I love it too much to leave it."

★ ★ ★

Driving west from Chimney Rock, I spot a small sign directing me to Rebecca Winters's grave. I don't think; I just turn the wheel sharply to the right, directing us toward a tree-lined patch off the road.

In the months leading up to our trip, I'd regularly come across information on Rebecca Winters, the Mormon emigrant who in 1852 began the 1,200-mile journey west from Nauvoo, Illinois, to the Salt Lake Valley. Like many Latter-day Saints, Rebecca, her husband, Hiram, and their four children aspired to a new life in the West—one free of the religious persecution their fellow Saints had faced in Illinois, Missouri, and Ohio.[7] That June the Winters family joined the James C. Snow Company and began their journey to what LDS president Brigham Young believed to be the promised land.

Everything seemed to be going well at the start. But soon illness struck many in the wagon train, including fifty-three-year-old Rebecca, who suffered a bout of cholera in mid-August and died days later. She was interred in the Nebraskan soil, a wrought iron wagon wheel placed atop her grave.

Decades passed, and eventually, Rebecca's grave was all but forgotten. Were it not for surveyors for the Burlington Northern Railroad, it might've been lost good. But in 1899 the surveyors uncovered her grave, prompting them to reroute the rail line ever so slightly to ensure that Rebecca's grave remained undisturbed.

For nearly a century trains shrieked past her grave, until 1995, when with the permission of Winters's descendants, Rebecca's body was exhumed and reburied one hundred yards from the original site—a safety measure to ensure that visitors like us refrained from getting too close to the tracks.

As I park, I'm surprised to find that Bullseye isn't the only vehicle in the lot; a giant RV takes up most of it.

"Is this Scotts Bluff?" Henry asks, well versed in the day's itinerary.

"Nope." I say. "This is Rebecca Winters's grave."

"Who's Rebecca Winters?"

"Well, she was a wife and a mom and a Mormon emigrant—" I begin.

"Let me guess," he interrupts, having heard this story before, "but then she died."

"Yeah, buddy, I'm afraid that's how this story always ends."

As we approach the grave, I spot a couple in their sixties, a woman in her thirties, and a few young children scampering about. We weave our way through them, offering smiles and waves as we make our way toward the gravesite. Admittedly, it's a strange way to spend one's time—hunkered alongside an emigrant grave in windswept Nebraska. That we are all here puts me at ease, though I can't help but wonder: why are we all here? I have my pseudo-scholarly reasons, of course, but what is the other family's excuse?

I turn toward the older gentleman alongside the grave and introduce myself.

"Roger Castle," he replies.[8]

"So, Roger," I say as casually as one might, "what brings you to Rebecca Winters's grave?"

"Well," Roger begins, "she was my great-great-great grandmother."

16. Paying respects to Rebecca Winters, Scottsbluff, Nebraska. Courtesy of the author.

My eyes grow as big as wagon wheels.

"Wait," Henry intervenes, "so you're her—"

"So she's your—" I continue.

"Great-great-great grandmother," Roger repeats.

I run through the countless scenarios in which this encounter might've never occurred. If we'd stopped for gas, for instance, or hit a stoplight or taken a bathroom break. It all seems a little too good to be true. For perhaps the first time in history, three generations of Rebecca Winters's descendants have gathered to pay their respects. And by some cosmic calculus, Henry and I are here to witness it.

"What's it like," I ask, "to visit your great-great-great grandmother's grave?"

"It's awesome," Roger says. "But I've been here before." He nods to his daughter, Rachel, who listens from just a few feet away. "We brought her when she was a young child. And these are her children," he continues, pointing toward his grandchildren as they zoom around the RV.

"So . . . this is a pilgrimage of sorts," I say to them both.

Rachel nods, sidling toward us. "I was about thirteen when I first came," she says.[9]

"And you remember it?"

"Oh, I definitely remember it," Rachel says. "It's one of those things that always stayed with me."

"This place reminds us of the sacrifices people made when traveling west," Roger says. "We bring our kids and grandkids here to remind them that life wasn't always as it is today."

I smile as Roger's eyes flitter from his daughter to his grandchildren.

"It's my understanding that the Mormon emigrants were incredibly disciplined," I say. "That your ancestors were the envy of the western-bound wagon trains."

"It was a cooperative group," Roger confirms. "They had a shared purpose."

While many nineteenth-century emigrants joined wagon trains to see themselves safely to the West, members of the Church of Jesus Christ of Latter-day Saints remained ever mindful of the wagon trains coming after them. Bound by their religion, they felt an obligation to look out for their fellow Latter-day Saints, Roger explains.

"It wasn't every man for himself," Rachel says. "It was a community effort."

In *The Gathering of Zion* Wallace Stegner wrote that the Mormon emigrants were "the most systematic, organized, disciplined, and successful pioneers in our history."[10] It's no overstatement. Excepting a few handcart company expeditions (more on that later), the nineteenth-century Mormon emigrants outperformed their non-Mormon counterparts again and again. It was never easy, and lives were lost, but they endured.

"And that's one of the important lessons too," Rachel says, "teaching our kids that they can do hard things just like our pioneer ancestors."

"They were people, and we're people," Roger says. "It's not like they were superhuman."

"It was a choice," Rachel says. "Some Mormons chose to stay back and not to follow Brigham Young to Salt Lake, and that was definitely easier. But others chose to follow their faith. And that's what I was just telling my kids a few minutes ago. How at some point you're going to have to make that choice too: you'll have to follow your faith or choose something easier."

Henry, who's been balancing against the metal posts surrounding the grave, takes a sudden interest in our conversation. So much of our trip has been about choices—visiting this instead of that, eating here instead of there—and at every turn we've weighed our options endlessly. But we've yet to find ourselves at any crossroad like those the emigrants endured. Not once have our decisions had such high stakes, nor have we had to rely on faith to make the right call. I'm ashamed to admit that this far into our journey, our idea of "prayers being answered" has generally involved gas stations with slushy machines.

Yet for the God-fearing emigrants, unanswered prayers could mean a death sentence. When supplies ran low and diseases ran high, sometimes prayer was all they had.

"When you look back at these people," Rachel says, nodding to her great-great-great-great grandmother's grave, "you can't help but think, 'Could I be Rebecca Winters?'"

★ ★ ★

Waving goodbye to the Castle family, Henry and I continue on for seven miles, until Scotts Bluff comes into view. The towering, eight-hundred-foot-tall chunk of sedimentary rock stands stately above the town of Gering, Nebraska. Though its bluff face in no way resembles Chimney Rock, I can't help but compare the geological wonders. The emigrants felt similarly. According to emigrant Joel Palmer, Chimney Rock resembled a "hay stack with a pole," while emigrant Asahel Munger described Scotts Bluff as "an old castle with a rounding top."[11] I agree with both men's assessments. Though for a twenty-first-century opinion, I turn to geologist Keith Heyer Meldahl, who distinguishes between the two by claiming Chimney Rock "the most sublime" rock formation along the trail and Scotts Bluff "the largest and grandest monument of all."[12]

17. Standing in the shadows of Scotts Bluff National Monument, Gering, Nebraska. Courtesy of the author.

The closer we get to Scotts Bluff, the larger and grander it seems. After paying the entrance fee, Henry and I begin the winding drive up the rock; Bullseye and his 180-horsepower engine easily managing the steep grade to the top. We park, then dig through our food bag for something resembling lunch.

I scrounge smashed bread, a warm jar of peanut butter, and jelly packets and make the obvious culinary suggestion: "PB&J?"

"Oh yeah," Henry agrees.

We round out the meal with a side of potato chips and a blueberry muffin snagged from the morning's continental breakfast. And to wash it all down: thirty-two thirst-quenching ounces of a fruit punch–flavored sports drink.

We take our seats on a bench overlooking the expansive view below: a speckling of pine trees and farmland engulfed by a canopy of sky. Dressed in his Captain America tank top and matching plaid shorts, Henry looks every bit a six-year-old. Meanwhile, the newly emerging crow's-feet beneath my eyes make me look every bit thirty-four. But the altitude—as well as our unexpected run-in with the Castle family—rejuvenates me. Suddenly I am alive and aware of my aliveness. How rare a gift to be both, and what better than a million-year-old bluff to do the reminding?

"What do you think about when you see all this?" I ask Henry through a mouthful of peanut butter.

"My sister."

"Really?" I ask, more than a little surprised. "You must really miss Eleanor, huh?"

"No," Henry's quick to correct. "I just think she'd probably want to jump down this cliff, even if you told her not to."

"Well, perhaps," I laugh.

But the truth is we're both beginning to miss our people.

Off to our right I spot a family of four: a mother, father, and a pair of teenagers bickering over a quarter-fed viewing station.

"It's *my* turn," the brother says, giving his sister a shove.

"You already had your turn!" she fires back.

"Do we have any more quarters?" the father asks wearily.

"We've used plenty!" the mother snaps.

If Eleanor and Meredith were with us, I imagine we'd be waging a similar war. But since we are, for once, not the ones making the scene, we enjoy our front row seat to the action: munching our PB&Js as the fight enters its second round. The mother's voice rises as her teenagers jam their scowling faces into the binocular holes, spinning the viewing station on its swivel. I try to get a read on the father, who, like me in these situations, seems to have faded from the scene. A slight smile materializes across his face as he stares up at the clouds.

Maybe, I think, *he's dreamed himself to Tahiti.*

I try to catch the father's eye to give him the ol' "Been there, buddy." But it occurs to me that I haven't. In fact, I have no earthly idea what it's like to raise two teenagers. All I know is what the emigrants knew: that when venturing down a path for the first time, it's best to proceed with caution. And if you've got it in you, a hint of humility too.

"I'll look first, then you can look," the brother suggests.

"No, *I'll* look first," the sister says, "then *you* can look."

I keep my mouth shut, though the irony is obvious: amid all the bickering everyone misses the view.

* * *

We eat, we hike, we steer clear of viewing stations, and after two hours of rabbits and mountain flowers, Henry and I are back on the road.

Next stop: Fort Laramie—the second of the major forts along our route.

We've barely made it a few miles down Nebraska Highway 92 before I realize I'm doing it again: blurring past one small town after another without even coming close to making a memory. Mostly, all we make are dust clouds, bypassing the one-stoplight towns without so much as a glance out the window. After speeding through Morrill (population 908), I tell myself to do better: to slow down, take a breath, and try harder to see what I've been missing.

Eight miles later I spot a sign I can't possibly overlook.

"Henry!" I holler, pointing to it off to the right.

"What?"

"No, that's the name of this town! We're in Henry, Nebraska! They must've named it after you!"

Of course, Henry knows better than to believe me. After all, even a place as small as Henry—just over a quarter-mile in total land area—would never take its name from some kid.

Except it did.

The story of Henry, Nebraska, begins twenty-seven years before the town existed. It begins in 1882, when Yorick Nichols—a cowboy and cattle raiser from Pennsylvania—journeyed west to our present location. Shortly after his arrival, he purchased five thousand acres of land and upon it worked to create a life for he and his wife, Alice, along with their adopted son, Henry Dyer.

Beyond that little is known of their lives. One source noted that Yorick "keeps as one of his most prized relics his father's commission as a captain in [Winfield Scott] Hancock's corps of the Union army, signed by President Abraham Lincoln."[13] And that Yorick's wife, Alice Dyer of England, was "a woman of literary talent who did quite a little writing." But that's where their trail runs cold.

Even less is known of young Henry. His story ended at around 8:00 p.m. on August 4, 1908, when the thirteen-year-old went for a swim in the North Platte River across from the family home. He was joined by a couple of friends, all of them enjoying themselves until the night turned deadly.

They found young Henry's body the following morning, tangled among the weeds in the spot where he'd last been seen.

"The boy was nearly fourteen years old," Henry's obituary reads, "and was popular among his playmates and neighbors."[14]

Heartbroken, Yorick and Alice attempted to honor their child the best way they knew how: ceding a portion of their property to the Lincoln Land Company, which assisted in creating a village. Their only stipulation: that the village be named Henry.

Months after its founding in 1909, Yorick served as the village's first postmaster. With each letter addressed to Henry, Nebraska, the grieving father surely thought of his son.

None of this is known to us as we pass through the town. Later, when I learn of the tragedy, I'll try to bear its weight. But it's impossible. The distance between the joy I felt while traveling through Henry and the grief Yorick felt while naming it is a chasm I don't dare cross—even hypothetically.

Yorick paid too high a price for the lesson that I now learn secondhand: that none of us can love our children enough to guarantee their safety.

I glance in the rearview to find Henry sketching in his composition book.

I reach back and tousle his curls, just to make sure he's still there.

★ ★ ★

Half an hour later, when we pull into the parking lot at Fort Laramie, Henry hops from the car happy and healthy. Ahead of us

18. The barracks at Fort Laramie, Laramie, Wyoming. Courtesy of the author.

we see the fort much as the emigrants did: the cavalry barracks, the store, and the commissary stretched just ahead of us. On the hill to our left we spot a Stonehenge-like structure, the ruins of the old hospital, where lives not wholly unlike our own were lost and sometimes saved. Surrounding the square are the captain's quarters, the officers' quarters, the infantry barracks, among other buildings. In all, eleven of the original structures remain—many of them restored and refurbished—making it easy for Henry and me to envision the fort as it was in its heyday between the 1850s and 1870s.

The history of Fort Laramie is long, convoluted, and with no clear starting point. Though 1834 serves as one beginning (the year in which frontiersmen Robert Campbell and William Sublette established the region's first fort, Fort William), we might also point to 1841 (the year Fort Platte was built—a rival trading post just a mile away).[15] Such blatant one-upmanship demanded that the owners of Fort William respond, which they did by building a bigger and better fort, Fort John, which was purchased by the U.S. Army in 1849. At which point Fort John was renamed Fort Laramie, which is how we know it today.

None of that is of much interest to Henry and me, who find ourselves—much like Loren Pospisil back at Chimney Rock—more curious about the stories of the people than of the place. Though in the case of Fort Laramie, trying to extricate one from the other is a fool's errand, as park ranger Steve Fullmer informs us as we follow him to his office in the back of the commissary.[16]

"Sorry for the mess," Steve says, leading us toward a couple of chairs. "We don't require anyone to wear a hardhat back here, but we should."

After thirty-nine years Steve holds the record for longest-serving employee at Fort Laramie, over which time he's accumulated a staggering amount of knowledge on all things fort related. When I ask what makes this fort unique compared to the others along the route, Steve explains that it all has to do with location. The fort's fortuitous placement at the confluence of the Laramie and the Platte Rivers has made this patch of land a popular gathering spot for humans since the Paleoindian period—somewhere between eight thousand and twelve thousand years ago.

Much like Fort Kearny, Fort Laramie supported both trade and military purposes, though it also served as a cultural center. Following the decline in the beaver trade in the late 1830s, the region's more capitalistic-minded men formed new partnerships with Native American tribes—most notably the Lakota—to trade buffalo hides to a growing market.

"Buffalo robes were the new brown gold on the plains," Steve says. "But fur traders didn't go out and kill buffalo. Native Americans went out and killed buffalo, and the fur traders traded for them."

Given the fort's placement on the Platte as well as its proximity to both Native American tribes and the buffalo themselves, Fort Laramie became the ideal location for such business transactions. And through these transactions, culture was exchanged as well.

"One of the things that's most amazing to me—and it was right there in front of our eyes—is the realization that fur traders and Native Americans interacted and literally created a mixed-blood population," Steve says.

Yet over time the resulting population fell out of favor with both groups. Once considered a vital link in the fur trade due to their tribal-white connections, this biracial population soon became, as Steve puts it, the "pariahs of the plains." Neither white people nor Native Americans were willing to accept them fully, thereby forcing them to live on the periphery of both worlds.

For Steve this mostly overlooked facet of history complicates our understanding of Fort Laramie. "If you come to this place as a visitor or historian, you think, 'Okay, there's the fur trade period, the military period, the emigrant period.' Everything has its nice little box. But after a while you realize that the very thing that makes this place so important is that it was this giant mixing bowl of cultures coming together: making peace, breaking peace, all on this little bitty spot of ground."

Fort Laramie's history, like America's history, is not without its complexities. While the fort served as the site for several treaties, these treaties varied in effectiveness. In 1851 eight Native American tribes—the Arapaho, Arikara, Assiniboine, Cheyenne, Crow, Hidatsa, Mandan, and Sioux—joined the U.S. government in signing the Treaty of Fort Laramie, which strove to clarify territorial claims between the various tribes while also guaranteeing safe travel for Oregon Trail emigrants passing through particular corridors.[17] The treaty failed on all fronts: peace between the tribes was soon broken, and emigrants—many of whom now had a gluttonous thirst for gold—could hardly be contained to corridors.

The 1868 Treaty of Fort Laramie was even more ambitious, calling for—among other demands—an end to war, the creation of the Great Sioux Reservation, land allotments for tribal farmers, and a promise from the U.S. government to provide tribes with doctors, teachers, carpenters, and other highly sought professionals.[18] Unsurprisingly, this treaty, too, failed to live up to its expectations.

19. F. M. Sargent's cabinet card of Nez Perce leader Chief Joseph and his family in exile, circa 1880. Washington State History Museum, via Wikimedia Commons.

Chief Joseph of the Nez Perce tribe remembered his father, Old Chief Joseph, wisely resisting such treaties. "He claimed that no man owned any part of the earth," Chief Joseph remarked, "and a man could not sell what he did not own." Old Chief Joseph was acutely aware of the damage that could be inflicted by the stroke of a pen, warning his son, "When you go into council with the white man, always remember your country. Do not give it away. The white man will cheat you out of your home."[19]

In 1868, during a council meeting at which Old Chief Joseph was not in attendance, such sage advice went unheeded by a fellow Nez Perce chief, who—whether it was within his authority or not—signed away much of their lands.

Three years later, as Old Chief Joseph lay on his deathbed, Chief Joseph took his father's hand and listened carefully to the great man's final words. "This county holds your father's body. Never sell the bones of your father and your mother." For six years Chief Joseph protected their land as best he could. But in October 1877—after leading his people on a 1,400-mile march from eastern Oregon toward the Canadian border—they were at last surrounded by U.S. forces. Faced with no alternative, Chief Joseph surrendered in the Bear Paw Mountains in the northern Montana Territory.

"I am tired of fighting," Chief Joseph was said to have proclaimed to the U.S. general, adding later, "My heart is sick and sad." Chief Joseph closed with a line that would long be remembered. "From where the sun now stands I will fight no more forever."[20]

Such "farewell speeches" became their own genre, one Native American after another offering lamentations for a way of life that seemed to be fading before their eyes. Chief Black Hawk of the Sauk tribe delivered his own farewell speech in 1838, followed by Chief Seattle's in 1854, followed by Chief Joseph's aforementioned speech in 1877. There were many more in between, America's indigenous people putting into words the horror that had been wrought upon them. While the speeches differed somewhat in message and tone, there's no mistaking their shared through line of grief.

One of the most devastating firsthand accounts of the cultural decimation of Native American life was offered by an unnamed tribal elder in an unknown year in the days leading up to his death.

"My sun is set," the elder said. "My day is done. Darkness is stealing over me. Because I lie down to speak no more I will speak to my people." The elder went on to describe a time when hunting grounds "stretched from the Mississippi to the mountains." A time when he and his fellow tribespeople were "free as the winds and heard no man's command."

But that time had passed.

"Then the white man came to our hunting grounds, a stranger . . . They took away the buffalo and shot down our best warriors. They took away lands and surrounded us by fences. Their soldiers camped outside with cannons to shoot us down. They wiped the trails of our people from the face of the prairies. They forced our children to forsake the ways of their fathers. When I turn to the east I see no dawn. When I turn to the west the approaching night hides all."[21]

The destruction of Native Americans' way of life might be traced to any number of congressional legislative efforts, from the Indian Removal Act of 1830, which laid the groundwork for the forced removal of tens of thousands of indigenous people from their ancestral home, to the Indian Appropriations Act of 1851, which allocated federal funding for the creation of reservations in the West. The combined effect was devastating, resulting in a no-win situation for the people who had prospered and thrived on that land for generations.

You needn't peer into a crystal ball to know what happened next. How quick on the heels of the Treaty of Fort Laramie (1868) came the passage of the Dawes Act of 1887—a government-backed effort to continue the assimilation of Native Americans while simultaneously taking their land. The Dawes Act authorized the U.S. government to survey and divide tribal lands for individual ownership, thereby diminishing collective ownership. The result was a loss of nearly ninety million acres of tribal lands between 1887 and 1934—land that white people were quick to claim as their own.[22] In addition, the shift from the communal holding of property to individual property fundamentally altered Native American culture, further pressuring indigenous people to adopt a more Euro-American model of living, one with the nuclear family—rather than one's tribe—at its center.

Which is to say nothing of the forced relocations.

The creation of Native American boarding schools in the late nineteenth century was yet another way to decimate indigenous culture, indoctrinating native children into a Euro-American lifestyle complete with Christian teachings, lessons on the English language, and—in an act that seemed to complete the forced transition—replacing the children's birth names with European ones.

Assimilation is one word for it; *cultural genocide* is another.

★ ★ ★

I am far from the ideal conveyer of this story. An estimated 90 percent of literature on Native Americans has been written by white people like me, leading to, as one scholar put it, "merely another example of the exploitative and unfair treatment of Indian people." Recognizing this truth, I hesitate to say too much. Yet to disregard Native American voices and perspectives seems another form of trespass. "To write a history of the Anglo-American experience is not wrong," the aforementioned scholar adds, "but to claim that it represents the entire history of the American experience is a gross mistake."[23]

Regrettably, it's a mistake we keep making. Such Eurocentric retellings of the "taming of the west" perpetuates a carefully curated, whitewashed view of history. One that, when spun in its usual way, only reinforces the American mythos surrounding the emigrants' intrepid explorations while conveniently overlooking the ravages left in their wake. But the emigrants themselves needn't shoulder the blame alone.

After all, it was the U.S. government and its military—by way of deception, manipulation, threats, and massacres—that provided the self-serving policies and systemic structures that allowed white people to claim land that was not theirs. When Native Americans attempted to broker peace with the United States, they were often told that the only way to attain such an end was to leave their ancestral lands and take up residence in a reservation of the U.S. government's choosing. The choice was clear: relocate or be killed.

The U.S. government created the conditions to make it appear lawful: wrote treaties, held councils, demanded signatures, and then stringently enforced whatever preposterous propositions they'd devised. Conflict was key. As such, the U.S. military utilized any minor violation of the treaties as grounds for further escalation.

"I would like to shake hands with the white man," remarked Little Raven, leader of the Arapahos, "but I am afraid they do not want peace with us."[24]

Little Raven was right.

Had the U.S. government sincerely wanted peace, they could have had it. But what they wanted was as much land as they could grab as expediently as possible. Not to mention the further submission of America's indigenous people.

Despite all this, to treat Native Americans as victims of history, rather than participants of history, is another misstep, according to Chimney Rock curator Loren Pospisil. In doing so, we dismiss Native Americans' many attempts to push back against the invading emigrants. America's indigenous people were not passive to the influx of emigrants. They responded to the threat as best they could, altering the course of history in the process.

* * *

A few hours later, after sharing a sarsaparilla in the Post Trader's store, Henry and I leave Fort Laramie and its history behind. Though, of

20. Retracing the Guernsey Ruts, Guernsey, Wyoming. Courtesy of the author.

course, we can never leave history behind: it lingers, loiters, haunts. As it should. I'm anxious to learn more of the Native American perspective of the westward expansion story, which we will, in a matter of days, when visiting Tamástslikt Cultural Institute in Pendleton, Oregon.

But for now we continue sixteen miles west of Fort Laramie to pay our respects to the Guernsey Ruts, the best geological reminder of the magnitude of the wagon trains. For folks like Henry, who struggle to understand the historical importance of the swales, there's no denying the jaw-dropping wonder of the ruts. Both swales and ruts send much the same message related to the tens of thousands of emigrants that once glutted the landscape, though the ruts serve as the most dramatic proof. And they're at their most dramatic in Guernsey, where the continual roll of wagon wheels left their impressions five feet deep in the sandstone.

Moments after disembarking from Bullseye, Henry's cowboy boots clip-clop along the rutted trails. Within minutes he's hip-deep in ruts, his red hat a flare in the distance.

"Wait up!" I call.

"I can't!" he shouts. "Mosquitoes!"

Suddenly they're everywhere—a maelstrom of buzzing bloodsuckers. In 1842 one emigrant complained of the "legions of mosquitoes" he'd endured in Nebraska.[25] Seven years later, in Idaho, an emigrant remarked that his horses and mules were so covered by the bugs that he could "scrape them off by handfuls."[26]

Today those legions and handfuls appeared to have relocated to Guernsey, their clotted swarms growing before my eyes. Henry and I swat at our all-but-invisible enemies, making little progress as they bob and weave just out of range. They lock in on us with military precision, their needle noses puncturing our skin.

We know when we've been licked. And so we raise our white flags, racing in reverse down the path as fast as we can for as long as we can before reaching Bullseye back in the lot.

"Well," I say breathlessly, slamming the door hard. "That was worth it, huh?"

"Are you nuts?" Henry asks, flicking an interloping mosquito from his arm.

"On to the campground?" I ask.

He nods wearily.

We can't get there fast enough.

★ ★ ★

After a long day on a dusty road, the KOA in Douglas, Wyoming, might as well be Disney World. We are treated not only to a western-themed miniature golf course but also a covered wagon jungle gym and in-ground pool to boot. It is our desert oasis. Our port in the storm. And best of all, there's not a mosquito anywhere.

Just when we think our prospects can't possibly improve, an angel's voice wafts from the loudspeaker.

"Just a reminder, folks, we'll be offering complimentary s'mores in the gazebo in a few minutes. Be sure to swing by!"

"S'mores?" Henry repeats. "Is this place for real?"

That night we play mini golf until the sun goes down, putting through nine holes and rewarding ourselves at the end of each with a generous slice of summer sausage. This is what passes for dinner, and since the sausage won't keep, we make short work of the entire log. I've made worse gastrointestinal decisions but not many.

We wash the sausage down with a fruit cup, some chips, and one water bottle each. Then, when it's too dark to see the holes, we return our balls and clubs, give the jackalope statue a pat, and begin the slow walk back toward the tent.

Darkness falls on Douglas at a few minutes before 9:00 p.m. It's a good excuse to make use of our flashlight, which we shine on the trail when we backtrack to the bathrooms a few minutes later. Side by side we brush our teeth, wash our faces, and take one more turn at the urinals.

Strolling back to the tent, an arm slung over my boy's shoulders, I think: *Today was a deathbed day.* Which is to say, it was a perfect day and one that—if the opportunity presents itself—I'll think back on in those final moments.

I wonder if Rebecca Winters was afforded such a comforting memory on her last day.

And I regret that Henry Dyer wasn't.

Because we can't stave off death, Henry and I stave off sleep, instead, slipping into our sleeping bags and reaching for our dog-eared copy of our new favorite book: Louis Sachar's *Sideways Stories from Wayside School.* I'd snuck the thin paperback into Henry's bag the night before we left. Just in case we needed a little light reading.

Turns out we did.

"So who's story should we read first?" I ask, flipping from back to front.

"Sammy's . . . no . . . Deedee's . . . no . . . Miss Zarves's!" Henry says.

"But we just read all of those last night!" I reminded him.

"Once more from the top then!"

Sighing, I clear my throat, hand him the flashlight, and flip to the opening page.

"'Chapter one, Mrs. Gorf . . .'"

When our eyes grow heavy, we whisper our nightly prayer.

Now I lay me down to sleep, I pray the Lord my soul to keep, if I should die before I wake, I pray thee Lord my soul to take. Amen.

Henry yawns, then pats my head twice.

"Night, bud," he says.

"Night, bud," I say.

I fall asleep to the sound of his snores.

21. Henry's illustration of the cave. Courtesy of the author.

5 Proceed with Caution

One death . . . occurred . . . far out under the mountains. Here the loose riders of our moving camp gathered one morning to examine a rude pyramid of stones by the roadside. The stones had been planted firmly in the earth, and those on top were substantially placed, so that the wolves, whose marks were evident about the pile, had not been able to disinter the dead. On one stone, larger than the rest, and with a flat side, was rudely engraved: J. Hembree—and we place it here, as perhaps the only memento those who knew him in the States may ever receive of him. How he died, we of course cannot surmise, but there he sleeps among the rocks of the West, as soundly as though chiseled marble was built above his bones.

—Matthew C. Field, 1843

MONDAY, JUNE 11
WEATHER: STILL HOT
RATIONS: WE SPRING FOR A COUPLE OF RESTAURANTS
DOUGLAS WY → BAR NUNN WY

At dawn I wake to shafts of sunlight slipping through the tent. The dew-soaked grass drenches my bare feet as I stumble sleepily to the campsite's picnic table, unfolding the map along the wooden planks. Today's our shortest drive yet—a fifty-mile straight shot from Douglas to Bar Nunn, a small town (population 2,785) just a few miles north of Casper. En route I've arranged to spend time with Randy Brown, an Oregon-California Trails Association member with an expertise in emigrant graves.

Though hundreds of thousands of overland travelers successfully made the journey to the Willamette Valley, over a quarter-century around sixty-five thousand didn't. Which is why the Oregon Trail has earned its nickname as "the nation's largest cemetery."[1] Though emigrants perished in any number of ways, disease remained death's closest ally. And of the many diseases the emigrants were exposed to along the trail, cholera wielded the scythe most expeditiously.

What was the cause of the dreaded disease?

Human feces. Specifically, human feces that had worked its way into the water supply. Though the ravages of cholera were hardly limited to nineteenth-century overland travelers (America's cities were hit too), indeed, the emigrants' journey provided the ideal conditions for the disease to flourish. "Given the lack of cleanliness and hygiene on the trek West," one scholar writes, "it is not surprising that a disease that thrives in human filth would start and spread as easily as it did."[2]

The "Unseen Destroyer," as it was often called, could cripple even the strongest emigrant within minutes. One historian described how stealthily it could "creep into the lungs on a spring breeze, or linger on the tip of a drinking cup, or come into the body via a goodnight kiss of a child."[3]

After that it was only a matter of time.

"The first symptom invariably is a stomachache," the historian continued. "The pain goes from zero to intense in a matter of two or three minutes. This is accompanied by diarrhea and vomiting. Not even assumption of the fetal position can bring relief. Dehydration becomes evident within hours, and the skin draws in, wrinkles and glazes. Cheeks sink in and eyes bug out, and a slight bluish cast covers the entire body, especially the fingernails."[4]

As horrific as death-by-cholera could be, nineteenth-century "treatments" were nearly as grisly. There was always "bleeding," of course, followed by a laudanum chaser. But there were more creative treatments, too, including "tobacco smoke enemas and hot water enemas infused with tobacco smoke or pepper." Yet the prize for the most peculiar treatment goes to the president of the New York State Medical Society, who in the 1850s determined that the best way to halt cholera-induced diarrhea was to plug the rectum. Beeswax or oilcloth, he determined, were typically up to the task.[5]

Today treatment is much simpler. One need only provide the afflicted with the necessary oral rehydration therapy—a solution of water, salt, sodium bicarbonates, and sugar—to minimize cholera's dehydrating effects.

"The most intriguing fact, to me, about cholera on the trail is that most parties probably had access to the necessary ingredients [to treat it]," cholera expert Roger Blair recently told me. All they lacked, he explained, was "the knowledge of what caused the disease, its mechanism of action, and how to treat it."[6]

Had the emigrants known then what we know now, tens of thousands of lives might've been saved. But since they didn't, Randy Brown has quite a job on his hands.

* * *

Cholera was one way to die on the trail, but it was hardly the only way. As the Hembree family learned all too well on Tuesday, July 18, 1843, when six-year-old Joel Hembree—while passing time balancing on a wagon tongue—slipped suddenly to the ground. In an instant his head was crushed beneath the wagon wheels.

Who can imagine the horror that followed? How Dr. Marcus Whitman came to the child's aid, only to determine that there was no fix for what had been broken. Dr. Whitman bandaged the boy's head, though it was no use. Within twenty-four hours Joel was dead.

His life story, short as it is, has long fascinated me.

Who was Joel Hembree besides the boy who died on the trail?

As is often the case in lives cut short (see: Henry Dyer), the details surrounding Joel's death far exceed the details of his life. His complete biography can be written in a single sentence: he was born to parents Joel and Sarah Hembree on March 2, 1837, in Warren County, Tennessee, and then, a mere 2,330 days later, died near La Prele Creek, just a few miles west of our campsite in Douglas.[7]

The surviving members of the wagon train buried him as best they could, employing a dresser drawer to serve as the top of the casket and piling tree branches beneath Joel's small body. While no fewer than five diarists make mention of Joel's death, none offer much in the way of details on the funeral. Unlike Sarah Keyes's and Rebecca Winters's well-documented funerals, all we know of Joel's is that it took place on the morning of July 20 and that the wagon train pushed on soon after.

Hours after that train rumbled on, twenty-three-year-old emigrant James Willis Nesmith stumbled upon the fresh grave as well as an accompanying note fastened to a stick. It read as follows: "Joel Hembree, child of Joel J. Hembree, aged six years . . . was killed by a wagon running over its body."[8]

I shudder at the pronoun.

* * *

Seventy-year-old Randy Brown arrives at our KOA at a few minutes before 9:00 a.m. Exiting his red SUV, Randy—dressed in slacks, a jacket, and a baseball cap—welcomes us to Wyoming. He's soft-spoken, mild mannered, and after exchanging a few words, he's back in the driver's seat of his vehicle. He tells me to follow him, that we'll be at Joel Hembree's grave in no time.

While it's not entirely uncommon to stumble upon the occasional emigrant grave along present-day western roads, you'll never "stumble upon" Joel Hembree's. His grave is too far off the beaten path, tucked deep into private land in Converse County. Private land that Randy has permission to enter.

As we drive deeper into that countryside, my eyes are drawn to dozens of flecks of fur in the distance. I know they're not pronghorns (America's answer to the antelope), though for miles Henry and I have marveled at those springy, tufted-tailed animals bounding alongside us. No, these creatures look different: larger, a little less springy, and lacking tufted tails. As we close the distance between us, the mysterious animals suddenly take shape.

"Bison!" I call. Henry sits up in his seat, squinting at the hairy beasts ahead of us.

"Holy cow!" he shouts.

"Not cows," I correct. "*Bison.*"

He rolls his eyes with the disdain of a well-seasoned teenager.

Aside from covered wagons, perhaps nothing better symbolizes the Oregon Trail than the American bison. Prior to their mass slaughter, the creature (also known as the American buffalo) had, for thousands of years, enjoyed a relatively carefree existence in the West. That changed with the influx of emigrants. Numbers vary, though at their peak in the 1500s an estimated twenty to thirty million bison were believed to have inhabited North America. By the late 1800s that number had shrunk to as few as five hundred. The species declined as a result of the usual human-induced reasons: a combination of habitat loss and unrestricted hunting.

Though I've seen my fair share of bison in zoos and wildlife preserves, I still struggle to describe them. What can one say other than that they are at once beautiful and terrifying?

"Great shaggy monsters," as one scholar described, "with protruding eyes the diameter of a teacup."[9]

Equally astonishing are the descriptions of their incalculably large herds. In 1845 one emigrant estimated that it took over two hours for a herd to pass, noting, too, the "immense gangs of wolves" who trailed just a short clip behind. In describing their movement, a fellow emigrant compared them to "Roman legions." They clopped along in "groups of paths, forty or fifty in number, about three feet apart, perfectly parallel."[10]

Weighing in between 750 and 2,000 pounds and measuring between six and twelve feet tall, the creatures made for an astonishing sight along the trail.[11] They cut a trim figure and were athletic, too, clocking in at forty miles per hour. As trail journals confirm, their bellows regularly erupted through the night, though not even their bellows compared to the sound of their stampede. Several emigrants likened it to "rumbling storms," though frequent trail traveler Ezra

Meeker compared it to a more recent noise to have entered the mid-nineteenth-century soundscape: "The roar we heard was like that of a heavy railroad train passing at no great distance."[12]

And then one day that roar turned silent.

Few factors contributed more to the decline of Native Americans than the decimation of buffalo herds at the hands of the emigrants. For the Native Americans of the Great Plains, buffalo were linked to survival. Old Lady Horse of the Kiowa tribe remarked that everything her tribe possessed, from tipis to clothing to moccasins, came from the bounty of the enormous creatures.[13] Not to mention that buffalo served as a major food source too. Little harm came from a wagon train's occasional killing of a buffalo; the problem was the commercialized, systematic slaughter of buffalo that occurred throughout the mid-1800s.

"Then the white men hired hunters to do nothing but kill the buffalo," Old Lady Horse remarked. "Up and down the plains those men ranged, shooting sometimes as many as a hundred buffalo a day. Behind them came their skinners with their wagons," Old Lady Horse continued. "They piled the hides and bones into the wagons until they were full, and they took their loads to the new railroad stations that were being built, to be shipped east to the market."[14]

To the Kiowas the buffalo was far more than a source of food and shelter. It served, too, as a mainstay of their religion. Annually, the Kiowa people took part in the Sun Dance, a religious ceremony that ended with a buffalo dance. As Old Lady Horse tells it, the sacrifice of a white buffalo calf was a part of the ceremony.

But what were they to do when the buffalo ran out?

"The buffalo saw that their day was over. They could protect their people no longer. Sadly, the last remnant of the great herd gathered in council, and decided what they would do," Old Lady Horse explained.

As Old Lady Horse tells it, one morning a Kiowa tribeswoman in present-day Oklahoma woke early to spot "the last buffalo herd appear like a spirit dream" through the mist off Medicine Creek. As the buffalo leader moved in the direction of a nearby mountain, his calves and cows in tow, something incredible occurred.

"As the woman watched," Old Lady Horse continued, "the face of the mountain opened."

It was the buffalo's last chance to return to the world they once knew, a home "green and fresh," where the rivers "ran clear, not red."

"Into this world of beauty the buffalo walked," Old Lady Horse said, "never to be seen again."

This is the true legacy of the bison: not that these "great shaggy monsters" once roamed freely along the plains but that we humans did what we often do—threatened a species' existence to suit our short-term goals. In doing so, the emigrants decimated native culture as well, reducing Native Americans' interactions with buffalo to stories and legends.

Were it not for a few forward-thinking nineteenth-century ranchers, we might've lost the American bison forever. Once those ranchers understood the depth of the devastation wrought upon the species, they tried to reverse course—capturing small herds of bison and breeding them back from the brink. Today a half a million or so can be found on private lands (such as the bison farm now before us) as well as another thirty thousand on public lands.[15] But of the tens of millions of wild bison that once inhabited the American West, a mere fifteen thousand remain free today. To put it bluntly, if you're looking for a home where the buffalo roam, you best keep looking.

Which is why Henry and I are grateful to see them at all. A herd of forty or so graze in the distance, their heads bowed as they sink their teeth into the tall grass, mushing it to cud. We drive past at a snail's pace, savoring every second with the hulking creatures, who seem like leftovers from some bygone era. Due to our ancestors' quick trigger fingers, in some ways they are. Peering out the passenger window, I try to extrapolate what twice that many bison might've looked like. Or ten thousand times as many. Though they are hardly the Roman legions I've read about, they are no less majestic. Just majestic on a different scale.

Leaving the bison behind, we follow Randy down a narrow stretch of road to our right. The road shrinks until it's hardly road at all, the dust giving way to dry mud and tire tracks.

"Come on, Bullseye, you got this," I say, and indeed Bullseye does, carrying us over the bumpy terrain. Randy parks in a patch of grass alongside a locked iron gate. I do the same. By now the bison have faded from view, as has the road itself. It feels strange to be so remote. Though by Wyoming standards, this is hardly remote at all. Yet for a guy like me (who's spent much of his life within spitting distance of hospitals and restaurants and every convenience known to humankind) the idea of being alone with my son and some guy I just met leaves me feeling a little unnerved. It's not that I don't trust Randy (he's one of the kindest and gentlest folks we've encountered the whole trip), but who can say what might go wrong?

Stepping from our vehicles, Randy says, "Mind opening my trunk?"[16] I do as I'm told, reaching inside the back of his vehicle to retrieve a large folder. I hand it to Randy, who slips his fingers into the folder's sleeve to produce a color photograph of a skeleton.

The skeleton of Joel Hembree.

"That's scary," Henry whispers, reaching for my hand.

"No kidding."

This photo exists because Joel Hembree's death wasn't, in fact, the end of his story. In December 1961 ranch hands accidently discovered Joel's grave alongside Le Prele Creek near Douglas, exactly where the boy had been buried 118 years before. Word of the then-unidentified gravesite reached trail historian Paul Henderson, who, after a bit of sleuthing in the trail journals, confirmed that the grave belonged to Joel. Joel's remains were found four and a half feet deep and were judged to be well preserved. In an effort to protect the grave from proposed construction on that parcel of land, Joel's remains were reinterred 1,625 feet to the west. Alongside Joel's body they discovered a pair of buttons—a reminder that the boy was more than bones. Once, he was a boy who wore a button-up just like Henry. And no doubt he had a favorite food, too, and a favorite toy and a favorite game to play on the plains. What little I know of Joel's personality comes by way of an 1884 account in the *Portland Evening Telegraph*, in which he's described as a "bright little lad" and "full of life and health."[17]

At least for a little while.

The strangeness of bringing my six-year-old to visit the grave of another six-year-old is hardly lost on me. In fact, it's all I think about as we trail Randy through the ankle-high grass.

What exactly are we doing here? I wonder. *Paying respects? Or simply trying to acknowledge the existence of a boy who's been mostly forgotten?*

For months I've agonized over Joel Hembree's story, occasionally waking in cold sweats at the thought of what he and his parents were forced to endure. Of the many deaths in the West that I've researched, Joel's hits me the hardest. It's not just the circumstances of his death that disturb me but that he died *here*, amid the wilds of present-day Wyoming. When his parents buried him, they knew there was little chance they'd ever return to his grave. The distance made any attempt all but impossible. Within a few years Mother Nature would surely reclaim the memorial.

Yet that we're approaching Joel's grave today confirms that wasn't the case. Thanks to Paul Henderson, Randy Brown, and others, Joel's memorial remains intact. But these future kindnesses were little comfort to Joel Sr. and Sarah Hembree, who on July 20, 1843, buried their boy and then left that place forever. Their quick and final departure was but the beginning of the indignities they and others faced when leaving a loved one behind on the trail.

We haven't yet turned to the subject of wolves, the trail's greatest graverobbers, who were notorious for unearthing bodies just hours after burials. Though just thirteen at the time of her travels in 1851, one emigrant long remembered the wolves serving as a constant threat to emigrant graves. "If there were any graves near camp we would visit them and read their inscriptions," the emigrant wrote decades later. "Sometimes we would see where wolves had dug into the graves after the dead bodies, and we saw long braids of golden hair telling of some young girl's burying place."[18]

22. Paying respects to Joel Hembree, Converse County, Wyoming. Courtesy of the author.

The emigrants protected the dead as best they could, stacking stones atop graves and flattening the dirt with their wagon wheels, though such precautions often proved to be a fool's errand. Many trail journals recount the horrors of discovering bone and fabric alongside the claw-scratched earth. Sometimes the wolves didn't even wait for the funeral to conclude before making their intentions known. They howled from the nearest hilltop, warning of the desecration soon to come. That the emigrants understood this to be the likely fate of their loved ones is almost too much to bear. What was the point of burial if their work was so quickly undone?

After a few leaps over streams, we arrive at Joel Hembree's grave. He's not alone but buried alongside two others—Private Ralston Baker, who was killed in a skirmish with Native Americans in 1867, and a former rancher who was laid to rest in 1994. They are a strange trio: three people who never knew each other in life but who are forever wedded by their shared burial ground near a creek in rural Wyoming.

As we approach the wood and wire fence that separates the graves from the wilderness, Randy grumbles that a little too much wilderness has slipped in.

"I got to do something about this grass," he says as we hunch low and slip through the fence. "I'll bring a Weedwacker next time."

"So . . . that's Joel back there?" I ask.

"Right here," Randy agrees, flattening the tall grass with his shoes and revealing a few stones beneath. My eyes focus on a bowling ball–sized stone upon which is engraved "J. Hembree."

Henry bobbles atop some nearby rocks, struggling to keep his balance.

"How are there no snakes here?" Henry asks.

"Oh, there might be," Randy says matter-of-factly.

Though the real danger—the invisible disease, the innocuous wagon wheel, the unseen wolves trailing behind the stampede—is the one you never see coming.

★ ★ ★

Fifteen minutes after leaving Joel Hembree behind, we arrive at a gate enclosing twenty-two thousand acres of private land.

"It's a little bumpy from here on out," Randy says, typing a code into a keypad. "It might be best for you two to ride along with me."

We heed his advice, parking Bullseye on one side of the gate and taking our seats in Randy's vehicle. It's a good thing. Less than a mile deep into that land, the road runs out completely. Or changes form, at least, to what I'll dub a rancher's road—a pair of tire tracks most suitable for Randy's all-terrain vehicle.

Out the window to our right, I spot a pair of wooden grave markers behind a metal fence.

"What do we got here?" I ask.

Parking his vehicle, Randy leads us toward the markers so he can tell the devastating story.

How on a July afternoon in 1864, a pair of Idaho-bound emigrant families—the Kellys and the Larimers—were approached by several friendly Sioux Indians in search of food.[19] Being well stocked, the emigrants shared a small portion, which pleased the Sioux, who, in exchange, escorted them farther west. But by nightfall the seemingly friendly band of Sioux had grown close to one hundred, far outnumbering the eleven members of the Kelly-Larimer train.

The attack came unexpectedly. While the emigrants prepared dinner, the Sioux warriors lifted guns and bows and killed several members of the party, including William Larimer, Reverend Andrew Sharp, Franklin Sullivan, and Noah Taylor, all of whom, Randy tells me, are buried beneath the marker to the left.

A few of the wagon train's survivors escaped, though Fanny Hurley, Sarah Larimer, and two children—seven-year-old Mary Hurley and eight-year-old Frank Larimer—were held hostage. They were mounted on a pair of horses and driven north, their fates seemingly sealed. In an effort to save her daughter, Fanny surreptitiously left scraps of paper in her wake, providing Mary a path back to the main trail. That night Fanny and Mary managed to escape together, though Fanny was quickly retrieved. Yet seven-year-old Mary remained hidden, following the trail throughout the night until spotted by three distant soldiers the next day.

Fearful that the young white girl was being used as a decoy, the soldiers refrained from attempting a direct rescue. Instead, they took a more circuitous route, losing sight of Mary in the process. When the Sioux spotted the soldiers, shots were fired, and the rescue attempt was aborted.

I wish this story ended happily, but since I know the grave to the right belongs to Mary, I know, too, how this story ends. Though Fanny, Sarah, and eight-year-old Frank would survive, Mary was found dead on the trail a few days later, her body riddled with arrows.

Staring at the grave, I think of both Joel Hembree and Mary Hurley—whose lives were cut short while traveling en route to some place their families had never even seen.

It was a high price to pay for a dream and one families kept paying.

"She was seven?" Henry asks, a tremor in his voice.

"Yeah, bud," I say.

Sighing, Henry turns back toward Randy's vehicle. I pray for better views ahead.

* * *

Leaving all signs of civilization in our dust, Randy drives us deeper into the wild.

"Where to?" I ask.

Randy glances at Henry in the rearview.

"Hey Henry," he says, "you want to see a cave?"

Since anything beats another grave, Henry opens his mouth to agree. But before he gets the words out, he shoots me his "Is-this-a-good-idea?" look.

Though over the course of a couple of hours, it's clear to us both that I've lost all sense of what constitutes a good idea.

Taking my son into a snake-infested wilderness?

Check.

Leaving our vehicle behind and entering someone else's?

Check.

Visiting the graves of two young children who died here?

Check.

Exploring a remote cave?

Why not?

About a mile deeper into the acreage, the road runs out completely. I keep my eyes on the horizon, but I don't see anything resembling a cave.

"Um . . . are we close?" I ask.

"Oh sure," Randy says. "Right over those hills there."

Hills, I'll add, that seem about a million miles away.

"Hear that, Henry?" I say, turning to face him. "Just over those hills."

Henry shoots me his "This-was-a-bad-idea" look.

Though eventually, those hills creep closer. We drive over them, parking at the bottom of a valley and stepping into the tall grass.

"Here we are," Randy says, unbuckling. Henry and I start our sure-footed walk behind him, keeping a close watch of every step as my ears grow attuned to all sorts of rattling.

Cicadas most likely, though there's no denying that we are now very much in rattlesnake country. To minimize risks, I position Henry just a foot ahead of me, figuring it's the safest spot: let Randy spook the snakes, while I keep an eye on our flank.

Worst-case scenario, I tell myself, *at least you had the good sense to bring along the snakebite kit.*

And the bad sense, I realize fifty yards in, to leave it in Bullseye's back seat.

But since our choices are few, we continue our ascent toward the cave, switchbacking in the grass as the terrain rises before us. Henry slips repeatedly, his cowboy boots no match for the loose rubble beneath him. Every time his hand lands on a sun-soaked rock, I see a ghost snake, fangs bared, shooting its scaly head toward his fingers. Since I can only endure so much of that phantom, I reach suddenly for Henry's midsection, then lug him football style the rest of the way. If the snakes want their pound of flesh, they'll have to settle for me.

"There it is," Randy says, leading us into the cave's wide mouth. I plop Henry down, and together, we enter into that darkness. Within seconds we note the dramatic drop in temperature, our sweat replaced with goose bumps. Once our eyes adjust, we view the full wonder of what's before us: a rock canvas complete with Native American pictographs, most of which are drawn in red ochre. One depicts a man wielding a tomahawk; another is of a man holding a shield. Animals line the walls as well—a rabbit, perhaps, among others whose shapes I am less certain to name. Most striking of all, however, is the pair of red handprints pressed to the rock face.

Whose hands were those? I wonder.

Alongside the pictographs are the scrawls of emigrant names. Some date back to the late 1800s, others later still. The names have mostly faded, though even the faintest lines serve as proof that they were once here.

Henry makes his way toward the back of the cave, past the pictographs, until he spots a few worn letters etched into the wall above his head.

"What's this one say?" he asks.

23. Native American pictographs, Converse County, Wyoming. Courtesy of the author.

I follow Randy across the dusty cave floor as we squint into the dark. "Kengstrom?" I try. "Kengitron?"

It's the middle letters that prove indecipherable, and after several failed attempts to come to consensus, we concede to the mystery.

"I don't think anyone's ever seen that one before, Henry," Randy says. "They had some archaeologists out here a while back, digging up the place, but I don't know if they saw that one."

Maybe he's being truthful, or maybe he's just playing along.

Either way Henry's eyes widen as he imagines himself joining the ranks of Marco Polo, Ferdinand Magellan, and Lewis and Clark.

"Buddy, you hear that?" I say. "You discovered something."

"I . . . discovered something," he repeats.

"You found Kengstrom," I tell him.

"I found Kengstom!" he shouts.

No matter who or what a Kengstrom is, sure enough, he found it.

★ ★ ★

We arrive at the Casper KOA in Bar Nunn, Wyoming, late in the afternoon.

The woman at the front desk runs me through the rules, including the most important of all.

"All trash," she says, "must be securely tied in bags before disposing of it in the trash cans."

"Really?" I ask. "Why?"

"Because," she says, "the wind!"

Five minutes later, as we attempt to stake down our tent, I more fully understand what she's talking about.

"Buddy, jump on the tent!" I shout as a thirty-two-mile-per-hour gust threatens to blow it away. Henry flings all forty-five pounds of himself to the nylon, splaying his body as wide as it'll go. Henry the Human Paperweight does his job admirably, buying me just enough time to pound a stake into the ground. From there I get to work inserting the poles, which, of course, now refuse to find their slots.

"Dad! I got sand in my eyes," Henry cries.

"Then close them!"

"I can't! They're full of sand!"

He runs, eyes closed, toward the water bottle on the picnic table, though, while en route, slams face-first into the site's slat-paneled windbreak. In all the confusion the tent tries to make a break for it, fluttering like a grounded flag from its three untethered corners.

An elderly man out walking his dog takes one look at us and says, "You fellas need help?"

"I think we're all set," I smile, laying prostrate on the ground.

"Well . . . okay then," he says uncomfortably, "if you're sure—"

I am not sure. But pride demands that there can be no other answer.

At last I coerce all four stakes into the ground. The nylon catches in the wind but for the moment holds firm. I wager there's a fifty-fifty chance our tent will be skirting across the sagebrush by nightfall, but we'll deal with that then.

For now we are in desperate need of being anywhere other than this dustbowl. Scanning the landscape, we spot a patch of grass at the limits of our field of vision: Antelope Park, a playground and baseball field adjacent to the KOA. As we make our way toward it, we stop to watch the players practice, sticking our fingers into the chain-link fence and listening to the clink of bats striking balls. It is music, or close to it, and I listen for as long as Henry allows before he drags me on toward the playground.

"Come on, Dad, play with me!" Henry calls, bounding up a climbing wall as he makes his way toward the slide. I huff and puff my way through what feels like a rigged obstacle course: stubbing my toe and hitting my head on most every outcropping of metal. I'm vanquished within minutes and, in an attempt to catch my breath, collapse onto the sunbaked slide. I doze off for a few winks, reawakening to the sound of those clinking bats.

"Daaaaaaaad," Henry calls, peering down at me. "Are you going to play or what?"

"Buddy, I'm trying," I say, standing. "Dad's just a little worn-out."

Henry's face drops.

"I wish I could play with kids my own age," he mumbles.

It hits me like a fastball to the chest. In all my fantasies of uninterrupted father-son bonding, I'd never fully considered the social cost. The isolation that comes with being a pair.

"I mean . . . you're great and all," he tries. "It's just that—"

"You're right," I say. "Sorry, man. I didn't really think this part through when I was planning the trip."

"It's all right," he shrugs. "It's no big deal."

His expression says otherwise.

Because I'm all he's got, I try to be the most that I can be.

"And you know what else I'm sorry for?" I ask, leaning toward him. "What?"

Rallying my energy, I slap his shoulder and sprint toward the slide. "That you're it!"

A toothy grin emerges.

"Not for long!" he calls.

If my huffing and puffing is any indication, I imagine he's probably right.

★ ★ ★

That night we escape to the big city of Casper. We need air-conditioning and sidewalked streets and a place where, when the wind blows, it doesn't feel like you're blowing away with it. Upon strolling beneath the marquee of a second-run movie theater, we make the impromptu decision to take in the 7:00 p.m. showing of some science fiction monster flick. The movie doesn't matter, only the comfy seats.

It's hard to imagine that just a few hours earlier, Henry and I had been wandering a cave with Randy. Or that just an hour before that, we'd visited Mary Hurley's and Joel Hembree's graves. That we are now seated in a cool, dark theater seems somehow impossible. A theater, I'll add, that's free of rattlesnakes and wagon wheels and every other danger.

But a few minutes into the monster movie, I realize we've now got bigger problems: a giant wolf trampling through a forest. Which wouldn't have been a big deal were it not for the scrolling text at the bottom of the screen placing that giant wolf in Casper, Wyoming.

Whoops go up throughout the theater.

"That's us!"

"There we are!"

How proud those locals are to watch their city's destruction!

Later that night, long after the movie ends, Henry and I cocoon ourselves into our sleeping bags. We beg for sleep, but the constant whir of semitrucks hurtling down U.S. 25 is hardly the lullaby we'd hoped for. Nor is the sound of the wind, which whips continuously against our tent.

That night Henry lays awake thinking of the giant wolf that, if Hollywood is to be believed, has descended upon Casper.

"Dad," Henry whispers sometime around midnight. "It was just a movie, right?"

"Right," I yawn. "No giant wolves to worry about."

"You sure?" he says.

"Sure, I'm sure," I say.

In the distance something horrible howls—wind or wolf, who can say?

"Um . . . Dad . . . ," he says.

"Night, bud," I say.

He shimmies a little closer.

24. Henry's illustration of Independence Rock. Courtesy of the author.

6 Recalculating the Route

July 7th. On top of Independence Rock. How often I have read and
thought about it, and now I am on top of it. The wind blows very hard.
That is the reason it is so unpleasant for those wearing skirts. It is
quite easy to ascend, but I think it will be more difficult to descend.

—Agnes Stewart, 1853

TUESDAY, JUNE 12

WEATHER: SEASONABLY WARM

RATIONS: PEANUT BUTTER SANDWICHES

BAR NUNN WY → ALCOVA WY → FARSEN WY → MONTPELIER ID

Since we are spared "death by giant wolf," Henry and I celebrate at
the top of the world. Or rather, at the top of a big chunk of granite.

Measuring in at 130 feet high and 1,900 feet long, Independence
Rock in Alcova, Wyoming, remains one of the most well-known
geological landmarks along the trail. Though it can't boast Chimney Rock's height or Scotts Bluff's square footage, it's covered
with emigrant names, forty to fifty thousand of which are etched
along its surface. Upon seeing Independence Rock in 1840, Father
Pierre-Jean De Smet bestowed it with the nickname "Register
of the Desert," and indeed it has served admirably in that role.[1]
Most every emigrant with a knife or axle grease left his or her
mark behind, reassuring those in subsequent trains that they were
still alive.

Which was no small feat. For those lucky enough to celebrate survival, many a glass was raised atop that rock. They'd

reached the halfway point in their journey—rattlers and cholera be damned.

Henry and I feel some vestige of the emigrants' excitement as we spot that rock through the windshield. We pull into the parking lot, then reach for our standard-issued provisions: a knapsack's worth of peanut butter sandwiches, chips, and a couple of water bottles. Since I can't hide my tourist tendencies, I embrace them, dangling both camera and binoculars around my neck like a pair of bandoliers.

"Did we forget anything?" I ask Henry. He's already out of earshot—his shoes pounding the paved path alongside the rock.

As Henry and I revel in the rock's natural surroundings, it occurs to me that we are the only ones here—a dramatic contrast to the Independence Rock of the 1850s, when this site was often a bustling metropolis. But that time has passed, leaving in its wake a few historical markers and an unobstructed view of the Sweetwater Valley. Seeing the valley for the first time, it steals my breath away: the whisper of the Sweetwater River, the sagging flowers in the sagebrush, and alongside it all, a colony of prairie rabbits peppering the landscape.

I'd designated two hours to complete the 1.3-mile loop—more than enough time to stop every fifty feet or so to admire the leaping pronghorns and the cud-chewing cows. But what I'll fail to grasp in that time frame is the full extent of Independence Rock's geological history. Its story begins over 2.6 billion years ago, a time when the world consisted of little more than rock and wind and rain.[2]

That we are witnesses to a geological wonder so long in the making proves to be among the more humbling moments of our trip. For some it is merely a rock, but when considering the time and conditions under which this rock was formed—the ancient granites that converged, the heating and cooling of molten rock, the pinballing of atoms, the countless eruptions and erosions and fissures and fractures—what can one say but thank you? Standing before Independence Rock, I am reminded of the words of Wendell Berry, who—while marveling at the age of the natural world and his place within it—remarked feeling "like a flea in the pelt of a great living thing."[3]

What a privilege it is to be a flea.

Three-quarters of the way around that rock, our hope for finding a trail to the top begins to fade. Henry, who never saw a rock he didn't want to scale, grows impatient.

"Didn't you say we were going to climb to the top?" he asks as we park ourselves on a bench.

"I did say that," I concede.

I hand him his sandwich as consolation.

"Then . . . why aren't we?"

Where to begin? Because the rock looks slick or because its crevices seem like a hotbed for snakes or—the most honest answer of all—because after visiting Mary Hurley and Joel Hembree's graves, risk avoidance is my primary mission.

I go with the answer that best shields me from the blame: the lack of trail.

"Why don't we just climb here?" he asks, pointing to the rock face directly before us.

"I don't know, buddy," I stall. "Let's just finish our sandwiches and see what's around the next bend."

He shoots me the second crushing look in so many days. Why can't I be the cool dad? The fun dad? The one who's unafraid to take the risk?

I'm not worried for my own safety but for his. Parenthood will do that to a person: making one's personal well-being a secondary concern. I don't dare mention this to Henry, who would counter the claim with such a multitude of *I'll be fine*'s that I'd lose all parental leverage within seconds.

But there's another reason I'm hedging on my earlier promise of hiking to the top. Today's risk averse decision-making is likely a direct response to my lack of it the previous day. The fates had granted us safe passage throughout our exploration of the cave—why press our luck? Then again, wasn't a willingness to press one's luck vital to the emigrants' success? But also: wasn't not pressing one's luck equally important?

There are no easy answers, only better views. And since we've come this far, it seems wrong to deny us the latter.

Before my more sensible self can prevail, I scramble up the side of the rock: hands down, waist bent, one foot in front of the other. I climb heart first into that rocky wilderness, pushing myself forward and refusing to look back.

When I finally do, I spot an ant-sized Henry far below.

"What the heck are you doing?" he shouts, his hands raised.

"I thought you said you wanted to climb Independence Rock?"

"I thought you said there's no trail!"

"I just made one!"

Grinning, he starts his slow ascent, hunched at the hips as his hands and feet propel him forward. Then he performs a crab-like shuffle, maintaining his low center of gravity. Once he gets the hang of it, he picks up speed, returning to an upright position as he strides confidently ahead.

He catches up with me within minutes, and soon we are half-running up that rock, our shoes defying gravity with their no-slip grip.

"Yee haw!" Henry calls as he bursts past me.

We are fifty feet from the top, twenty-five feet, ten, then five . . .

"We made it!" Henry shouts upon reaching the peak. "We made it without a trail!"

We share a sloppy high-five, a celebratory hoot. We gulp air as if breathing for the first time—long, steady breaths that we convince ourselves are somehow, better, sweeter, and cleaner than all the ones that have come before. With each exhale we sweep the cobwebs from our lungs, expelling the dust and germs that have been rattling within us since winter.

For fifteen minutes we explore separate sides of the rock, calling to one another to check out the various emigrant names still visible along its face.

"It's like they left us a message," I say, staring at the scrawls. "It's like they knew we were coming."

25. The view from the top of Independence Rock, Alcova, Wyoming. Courtesy of the author.

From our new vantage point we peer down at our country to see a truly specular view: one wholly free of humans. Maybe it's the solitude or the weight of history or that fresh Wyoming air—whatever the reason, I have never felt so close to my son. Not on the drive home from the hospital or the walk to his first day of school. Not during our annual trips to Lake Superior or when biking along the trail near the pines.

Of all the places we've been, this is the one we've been waiting for.

We will leave no mark upon that rock, though it leaves its mark upon us.

After ten minutes I say: "Well? Ready to head down?"

"Nah," he says.

"Okay," I say.

We stay for ten minutes more.

★ ★ ★

Sometimes leaving a place is a choice, other times less of a choice. Though it's true that most overland emigrants were motivated to go west for land and gold and opportunity, some sought freedom too. Religious freedom, in particular, as Rebecca Winters and her fellow Latter-day Saints can attest. After enduring violence in Ohio, Illinois, and Missouri, members of the Church of Jesus Christ of Latter-day Saints (LDS) continued their migration west. Under the guidance of Mormon president Brigham Young, between 1846 and 1868 some seventy thousand Mormon emigrants made the 1,300-mile trek from Nauvoo, Illinois, to the Salt Lake Valley.[4] Along the way they traveled through Iowa, Nebraska, Wyoming, and Utah, forming what we know today as the Mormon Trail.[5]

While the non-Mormon emigrants' primary concern was surviving the journey, as the Castle family made clear to me, the Mormon emigrants had a greater vested interest in those who came after. "The Mormon Trail was not a road of passage for random opportunists," one writer remarked, "but a permanent way prepared for the Gathering of Zion."[6]

Brigham Young's vanguard company of 1847 did much to pave the way for those who would follow. The group consisted of 148 Latter-day Saints divided among seventy-three wagons. They endured their fair share of difficulties but arrived in the Salt Lake Valley unscathed—every last Saint intact. It was either a sign from God, a bit of good fortune, or their reward for a well-executed journey. Whatever the reason, they'd made it. And if repeated with equal success, Brigham Young reasoned, then it was only a matter of time before the Salt Lake Valley would be overflowing with Saints.

In October 1851 Brigham Young issued a general epistle encouraging LDS members to journey to the valley as soon as possible.[7]

Not by wagons but by a far less-tested form of transportation: handcarts.

That's right, handcarts: two five-foot wheels connected to a platform and pushed or pulled by a pair of seven-foot poles. Their design provided Mormon emigrants exactly what they needed: lightweight transport that could carry between 250 and 500 pounds.

The handcarts weren't pulled by beasts of burden but by the Saints themselves—many of whom were new arrivals to America's shores, having emigrated from England, Wales, Scotland, and Scandinavia. They came rich in faith and short on money, hopeful that by answering Brigham Young's call, they would not only fulfill their religious duty but improve their own situations as well.

At its best the Mormon handcart migration worked spectacularly—a speedy and unencumbered method for overland travel. Logging an average of fifteen miles per day, the trip from Iowa City (where the Mormon train began) to the Salt Lake Valley could be completed in a lightning quick seventy days. But at its worst it was a disaster of epic proportions, one that claimed hundreds of lives. Much of this suffering befell the Willie and Martin handcart companies, both of which made the lethal mistake of striking out much too late in the season. Had they left in late May 1856, their journeys might have proven quite different. Yet delays demanded they leave two months later than planned, imperiling them in the process.

In some ways their story parallels another cautionary tale: the Donner-Reed party, whose own ill-fated journey a decade earlier, while less fatal, was no less horrific. Much like the members of the Donner-Reed party, the emigrants of the Willie and Martin handcart companies also endured shrinking rations, a blizzard blast, and by late October, a terrible reality: that they might not escape with their lives.

Brigham Young dispatched rescue parties, and by November a good number of the emigrants had been saved, though not before 200 or so Saints had been lost.[8] According to one scholar, the Martin company took the greatest hit, with an estimated 25 percent mortality rate, making it—in terms of overall deaths— the most catastrophic nonmilitary disaster on the westward trails.[9] Altogether, somewhere between 135 and 150 men, women, and children perished, never reaching the promised land they so desperately sought.

On November 4, when all hope seemed lost, members of the Martin Company huddled along the rocks of what we know today as Martin's Cove—a gigantic windbreak of sorts not far from the Sweetwater River. Their food nearly depleted, they were at the mercy of their rescuers, who, by the grace of God, arrived shortly thereafter. On November 9 wagons transported many of the suffering emigrants farther west. Days later they were met by additional wagons. By November 30 the Martin company survivors—excepting the twenty who stayed behind to guard the supplies—at last reached the Salt Lake Valley. Frostbite claimed more than a few fingers and toes, but it seemed a small price in exchange for survival.

Though Henry and I are no Saints, upon our arrival to the Mormon Handcart Historic Site later that morning, we're welcomed heartily by the site's many Mormon volunteers, two of whom agree to give us a tour of the property. They lead us toward a Kawasaki golf cart, then tell us to take our seats.

Along the way our guides point out various landmarks: streams, swales, wagon ruts. We've barely made it a hundred yards before a few pronghorns rise to their feet, bounding alongside us like a furry security detail.

Throughout the morning I'd grown accustomed to the landscape beyond Bullseye's window, though it hardly compares with the view from an open-air golf cart. The wind whips across our faces, Henry clinging tight to his hat for fear of losing it again. The tall grass bows in the breeze as we leave small dust clouds in our wake. Off to our right a granite ridge presses tight against the horizon. While it is all beauty and wonder on this sun-soaked day in June, I imagine a cold November morning—when food was scarce—when Mormon emigrants viewed the terrain quite differently: less something to admire than something to endure.

What makes the Mormon Handcart Historic Site unique is that it's more than some dusty old history lesson. Rather, it's living history. Each year tens of thousands of high school–aged Mormons return to this place to re-create the handcart treks of their ancestors. For

26. Mormon Handcart Historic Site, Alcova, Wyoming. Courtesy of the author.

a few days they're the ones pulling the handcarts, sometimes as far as twenty miles per day.

After ten or so minutes in the golf cart, we arrive at a giant rock a few hundred yards in the distance. It's not just any rock but Martin's Cove. We stare at the rock, which, in my inexpert opinion, seems the near-perfect size and shape for protecting emigrants from the elements. Nevertheless, it wasn't nearly enough. Though the rock blocked the wind, it could hardly fill a stomach or keep a body from freezing.

Though no diaries from the Martin's Cove expedition are believed to exist, those Saints who survived filled in the pieces of their harrowing plight. An English immigrant recounted the difficult days leading up to their worst trials, including the October day when he and his family were forced to cross the bone-chilling waters of the North Platte River. "It was very cold," the emigrant wrote, "and the next morning there was about 6 inches of snow on the ground and then what we had to suffer can never be told."[10]

The combination of shivering bodies and empty stomachs ravaged the Saints. One emigrant who discovered his father's frozen corpse beneath a wagon and whose mother was sick, noted plainly, "It seemed as though death would be a blessing."[11]

When Henry and I return to the visitor center, a volunteer encourages us to take a handcart for a spin. She guides us toward a track near the parking lot. Henry climbs into the back of a cart, then directs me toward the poles.

"Giddyap, Dad!"

Sighing, I retrieve the poles and begin careening us around curves. Within moments I prove myself to be the world's worst handcart driver. In my defense it's not easy—there's no steering wheel, no antilock brakes, and no engine other than me.

Yet somehow, between 1856 and 1860, three thousand Mormon emigrants covered the one thousand–plus miles in conditions far worse than the ones we currently face.[12] Driven forward by faith, many of them succeeded in reaching Zion. Who could have dreamed that human-pulled handcarts were capable of such a journey? And how successful the Willie and Martin handcart companies might've been—if only they'd left sooner.

★ ★ ★

After climbing Independence Rock and pulling a handcart, Henry and I are in need of a nap. But since we've still got three hundred miles of sagebrush ahead of us, we press on—grateful for air-conditioning and horse-powered engines.

While studying the map the previous night in Casper, I'd grown dismayed at the distance I'd expected us to cover in a day. Though our 534-mile slog from Clive, Iowa, to Doniphan, Nebraska, had proven to be the most grueling leg of our journey, our 340-mile trip from Casper to Montpelier, Idaho, comes in a close second.

In what universe did I think a six-year-old could endure such mileage?

It's one thing to cover that much country on our first joy-filled day of the journey, but now that we've reached day 6—nearly our halfway point—fatigue has begun to set in.

"Well," I say somewhere near a place called Muddy Gap, "I've got good news and bad news."

"What's the good news?" Henry asks from the back seat.

"The good news," I say, mustering every ounce of enthusiasm I've got, "is that we're stopping for ice cream at Farson Merc in a couple of hours!"

"And the bad news?"

"We still have a few hours after that—"

"*After* the ice cream?"

"I'm afraid so."

"So . . . you're telling me we have a few hours *before* the ice cream and a few hours *after* the ice cream?"

"Technically, yes," I say, "but it's only bad if you think about it."

"How do we not think about it?"

"Well . . . we could play Twenty Questions?"

He shoots me his weariest expression.

"Look, this isn't a hostage situation," I say. "We play a game, then we eat some ice cream. There are worse ways to spend a day."

Neither of us need mention Martin's Cove.

"Fine," he agrees. "But I'm going first."

★ ★ ★

Shortly before losing our minds ("Is it a vegetable? Animal? Cartoon character?"), Farson Mercantile appears on the horizon.

"Thank God," I say, pulling into the dusty lot adjacent to the two-story brick building. Most of the spots are filled, confirming the store's legendary status. As does the giant white placard welcoming us to Farson Mercantile, HOME OF THE BIG CONE.

Entering through the double doors, we turn left toward the ice cream counter. The endless glass counter displays a multitude of flavors—so many that, given Henry's commitment to thorough vetting, they will surely waylay us here all afternoon.

Which would've been fine had an irritable-looking line of people not formed behind us.

27. A much-needed detour for the Big Cone, Farson, Wyoming. Courtesy of the author.

"I hate to rush you," I say about thirty seconds in, "but we've got some company."

"I know what I want," he says firmly.

I am astonished. This from the guy whose indecisiveness makes Charlie Brown look like a well-oiled decision-making machine.

"Are you . . . sure?"

"Bubblegum and raspberry," he says.

"Two scoops, huh? So I guess we're going for a double then?"

"No," interrupts the young man working the counter.

"Pardon?"

"You're going to want a single," he says.

"Can we get two scoops in a single?" I ask.

"The single *is* two scoops."

"So you think the double will be too much for us?"

"Uh . . . yeah," the young man scoffs, giving us the once-over. "I'm pretty sure."

The competitive ice cream eater in me wants to take him up on the challenge. But since there's something to be said for humility (and limiting one's dairy intake), I relent.

"Fine," I say. "I guess we'll go with your single."

The young man gets to work, using more than a little forearm strength to heave two heaping scoops onto our cone.

"Well, it lives up to its reputation," I say, steadying the cone with both hands as Henry and I weave toward a picnic table directly beneath the HOME OF THE BIG CONE sign.

"Mind if we sit here?" I ask the woman across from us.

"Plenty of room," she says.

After a few minutes of conversation, the woman informs us that she's a resident of the nearby town of Green River.

"You said you're heading to Montpelier tonight?" the woman asks. I nod.

"Well, when you get a little way beyond that, you ought to consider stopping at Lava Hot Springs. It's a must-see. I took my grandkids there just last weekend."

She goes on to describe what to me sounds like some kind of Idahoan Shangri-La: an entire town built around water activities. "They've got a water park and tubing down the river and the hot springs, of course—"

"Dad," Henry says between frantic ice cream licks, "can we go to the hot springs?"

"Well," I say, "maybe we can revisit the itinerary."

My noncommittal *maybe* seems the least I can do given the 150 miles still ahead of us.

"So, what's it like living out here?" I ask.

The woman turns quiet.

"Listen," she says, leaning across the table, "you can't tell anyone about this place."

"It's that good?" I ask.

"Oh, definitely," she smiles.

She attributes most of her love for western Wyoming to its kind-hearted people but also the land's openness. She reminds me of the mountains and the rivers and the animals—all of which that state has in spades. She tells me, too, that Sweetwater County is in an ideal place to call home: just a few hours to Jackson, a few more to Denver, and a few more to Vegas.

"Long story short," she concludes, "we kind of have it all here."

I've heard similar claims from folks throughout our journey—that their place is the best place of all. And for those people it probably is. Ogallala is the best, and Kearney is the best, and Douglas is the best. If asked to share my favorite place on Earth, I'd probably pick my home too.

I can't help but love this woman's love for this land. And also her hope to keep it hidden.

"So, be careful what you write about us," the woman smiles, taking one last lick of her cone. "We wouldn't want this secret to get out."

★ ★ ★

One hundred and fifty miles later, after a second bout of highway hypnosis, a prairie dog shakes me from my stupor as he skitters across the road just outside of Montpelier.

Glancing at Henry in the rearview, I ask, "Are you as hungry as I am?"

"Starving," Henry agrees.

I turn right into Broulim's Supermarket. Aside from Farson Merc, we haven't entered anything close to a grocery since the Walmart in Sidney. To celebrate our return to civilized life, we strut through the automatic double doors. To our left is an ice-filled cooler overflowing with sports drinks, several of which we toss into our basket, our hands lingering in the ice longer than necessary. We are beyond hot and thirsty, and were it not for the security cameras, we'd have dunked our heads into that glacial coolness.

We walk every aisle of that store, marveling at the most basic items, which, after a week on the road, have taken on novelty status.

"Oh my God," I whisper, "are those . . . raisins?"

"Is that . . . candy?" Henry gasps.

Once the aisles run out, we make our way to the deli, where we order enough fried chicken and pizza sticks to feed most of Montpelier.

En route to the cash register, I snag a bag of grapes.

Henry lifts an eyebrow, confused by my impulse buy.

"In case Mom asks if we're eating fruit," I explain.

★ ★ ★

Upon checking into the Montpelier Creek KOA, we discover—much to our horror—that the place lacks a mini golf course.

"No mini golf?" Henry asks. "Then why are we even here?"

What it lacks in mini golf it makes up for with its in-ground pool, its playground, and its basketball court. The man behind the front desk, too, does his best to accommodate, assigning us a secluded campsite on the edge of Montpelier Creek.

Pulling into our site, we realize just how lucky we are. Of all the campsites—and we've had plenty—this one takes the prize. The creek flows ten feet from our tent, while just downstream, a wooden bridge offers easy access to a forest trail that spits us out near the playground. We have it all: creek and bridge and trail and playground. Though his short game might suffer, Henry makes peace with the lack of mini golf greens.

Here in Montpelier we are, quite literally, walking in the emigrants' footsteps. Historically, the Bear Lake Valley was a major stopping point for overland travelers, thousands of whom rested for a night or two directly alongside the creek near our tent. And that's just the start of the story. Before the emigrants, this land was traversed by a who's-who of well-known mountain men and explorers: from Jim Bridger to John C. Frémont. Tracing back further still are the region's original inhabitants, Native Americans from the Shoshone tribe, the Ute, and the Bannock. That we are now camping in listening distance to the creek that proved so vital to the survival of so many is as humbling as the view from the top of Independence Rock.

As Henry unfurls his sleeping bag inside the tent, I remove my shoes, then do my old-man shuffle into the creek just ahead of us. One wobbly step after another, at last I'm knee-deep into the frigid water.

"Can I try?" Henry asks. He's towering above me back on shore, his lucky hat tilted askew atop his head.

"Just . . . be careful," I say.

We take the risk together, wading alongside one another in the water as the stones and mud gather around our toes. When we can't stand the cold any longer, we retreat to the safety of the shoreline, taking our seats in the spindly grass to dry in the sinking sun.

Henry reaches for the nearest rock and tosses it into the water. The satisfying *plunk* sounds like history. I reach for one myself and give it a toss.

Plunk.

What starts innocently enough soon escalates to a highly competitive rock-skipping competition.

"Three skips!" I shout, hands raised victoriously. "Read it and weep, sucker!"

My trash talk only intensifies what once seemed a friendly competition.

Henry lands four skips, I land five, he manages six.

We skip and skip until all the rocks run out.

"Well," I say, "shall we call it a draw?"

"I guess."

Henry walks toward the picnic table and sets out two plates. He divvies up the food and cutlery, then places a Powerade alongside each of our spots. I watch on, silently.

"You ready to eat?" he asks.

"Yeah," I say. "I think I am."

* * *

The sun sets over the valley at 9:02 p.m. We watch from our place at the bocce ball court, where we've just invented a new game we've dubbed Basketball Bocce. It's exactly what it sounds like.

"Break left, break left," I shout, emulating the movement with my body. But the basketball refuses to break, opting instead to bounce clear out of the court and into the nearby mulch.

Just ahead of us, a pair of preteen boys reach for a baseball bat and crack balls deep into the distance beyond the creek. And theirs isn't the only bat on the premises. Above us we spot the winged variety as well, several of which dive-bomb and flutter overhead in an increasingly discordant dance. Nearby a mother and daughter play cards at a picnic table, while an old man readjusts his RV's satellite dish. A young couple walks back from the showers, their shoulders draped with towels. A man holds his cell phone skyward in search of reception. A woman cracks a beer by the fire.

By this late hour the pool has turned placid, the dogs have stilled, and the night sounds have emerged. My eyes turn to the laundry room connected to the campground store, which I take as a sign that perhaps we ought to make use of the facilities. After a week on the road, we've run perilously low on clean clothes.

"How do you feel about staying up past your bedtime?" I ask, nodding toward the washer and dryer.

"I feel good about it," Henry says.

I feed half a roll of quarters into the washer, then jam-pack the machine with every article of clothing we've got—underwear, socks, swimsuits, pants, and shirts. Everything we own is dusty or mud-caked or both. We're so low on pajamas that Henry resorts to wearing his

Ninja Turtle onesie for the second time of the trip—a fashion statement that sends me back to Doniphan on the night of the storm. My mind flashes to his attempts to hop himself into its foot holes as the wind and rain tore down. That night seems like a lifetime ago but also not.

Because it beats watching the suds of the washing machine, Henry and I leave the laundry room and spend the next half an hour wandering the grounds. Flashlight in hand, Henry leads the way. All of the sudden his leisurely stroll turns into a spontaneous sprint. Henry hurtles past the wooden bridge and into the forest, my four-foot-tall Ninja Turtle careening around the creek's many curves. He is punch-drunk giddy, panting and laughing as his body breaks through the spiderwebs on the ever-thinning trail. Since the darkness ensures that I can't make out anything ahead of me, I keep my eyes on the bobbing flashlight beam and try to trust my feet. Which is a lot to ask of one's feet on a dark night in a strange place.

Running along the trail behind Henry, I can barely make out that boy in his Ninja Turtle onesie. What I see, instead, is a boy bursting at the seams of childhood, a boy both literally and figuratively vanishing before my eyes.

After a couple of laps, it's clear he's got me licked. I double over for a few quick gasps of air.

"Hurry up, slowpoke!" Henry calls, somehow coming up from behind me. I turn, watch him blur past, then sigh and continue the chase.

Round and round, again and again, the distance growing between us.

* * *

That night we fold our clothes by flashlight. Afterward we gorge on fire-cooked s'mores. As tradition now dictates, we read *Sideways Stories from Wayside School* for as long as my eyes hold out. Only this time the creek's so loud that I have to shout just so Henry can hear.

When I crash, I crash mightily, waking at some unknown hour to relieve myself in the woods. I pee half-asleep, turning my eyes toward a cluster of stars overhead. For a flicker I imagine sailors using the same stars to guide them home. And maybe a few emigrants too.

I return to my sleeping bag, but this time I leave the tent flap wide. I've been separated from the world long enough, I determine.

From now on let the world come in.

28. Henry's illustration of the Water Bottle Incident. Courtesy of the author.

7 The Ghosts of Emigrants Past

I was astonished to see so much remaining of the land as it must have appeared to the emigrants in the middle 1800s. Along the mountain miles the snowy peaks reside in silent solemnity. Streams still flow. Prairie grasses bend to the winds.

—Ingvard Henry Eide, 1972

WEDNESDAY, JUNE 13
WEATHER: UNSEASONABLY WARM
RATIONS: TRUCK STOP DELICACIES
MONTPELIER ID → LAVA HOT SPRINGS ID → BOISE ID

While admiring the dawn from the picnic table, I'm interrupted by the all-too-familiar groans of the six-year-old still curled up in the tent.

"What's the problem, buddy?"

"Why can't the sun ever sleep in?"

"Well, it's sort of its job not to."

"It should get a new job."

"How'd you sleep otherwise?"

"Terribly," he says, rolling dramatically onto the grass. "It was that stupid creek. It was *so* annoying."

"I think the word you're looking for is peaceful."

We work through our morning routine—collapsing the tent, deflating the pads, and stuffing our sleeping bags back into their drawstring knapsacks. Each day I've tried to cede a few more responsibilities to Henry, which means by day 7 he's mastered the art of folding the tentpoles without poking anyone's eyes out. But amid all my lessons on wrapping and strapping and stuffing and packing, I'd overlooked a rather important one: watch where you sit.

"Ready to go?" Henry asks as he heads toward the car.

"Yeah," I chuckle, "but I'm not sure you are."

"Why?"

"You look like Peter Cottontail," I say, nodding to the tangerine-sized burr ball stuck to his backside.

"Peter who?"

"Buddy, you sat on some burrs."

He reaches a hand to his backside, sticking himself in the process.

"Dang it, Dad!"

"How is this my fault?"

"You could've warned me!"

"I just told you that you sat on burrs!"

"But you didn't say they were the prickly kind!"

"Turn around," I sigh, "let's get this over with."

One by one I pluck burrs from my son's butt with a surgeon's precision.

"Now hold still," I say as he spreads his hands against the car. "The more you squirm, the longer this'll take."

Though time seems to be of little concern to our camp neighbors, many of whom are enjoying their coffee while settling in for our show.

"Ouch!" Henry shouts.

"It hurts me too!" I shout back.

"Not as much as it hurts me!"

For the next five minutes we bicker over whom it hurts more—a much-needed distraction as I pluck every last burr.

"How's that?" I ask upon plucking the last one.

He offers a booty shake in answer.

"Well," I say, buckling up. "I hope you learned a valuable lesson."

"I did," Henry agrees. "Don't camp."

* * *

We've got an hour before our 9:00 a.m. interview with Becky Smith, the executive director of Montpelier's National Oregon/California

Trail Center, and so we drive up the road in search of breakfast. Off to the right we spot a sign for the Ranch Hand Trail Stop—a friendly-looking establishment complete with gas and grub. Since we need both, I pull over, filling the tank as Henry provides reconnaissance on the breakfast situation.

"How's it look?" I call.

He gives it two thumbs up and a lip lick—his highest recommendation.

Upon entering, we make our way toward a pair of stools alongside a stretch of counter. But before we sit, I notice a sign that reads: RESERVED FOR GRUMPY OLD MAN. Sure enough, the first five stools are, indeed, occupied by patrons who fit that description. Since a few stools still remain, Henry and I claim our seats on the opposite end, embracing our own inner grumpy old men.

"Morning guys," calls the waitress striding our way. "How we are doing this morning?"[1]

"Good," I smile. "How are you?"

"Great," she says. "My name's Shawneen. I'll be taking care of you. You know what you want?"

Her dark brown hair is pulled tight behind her, highlighting her hazel eyes. She's dressed in slacks and the standard-issue black Ranch Hand employee T-shirt, featuring a cowboy caricature head.

"Well, a coffee for sure," I begin, "and maybe the omelet special?"

Nodding, she turns to Henry.

"Pancakes," he says.

"Strawberries and whip cream?"

"Yes, please!"

No sooner does Shawneen disappear than I begin strategizing on how best to strike up a conversation with the grumpy old men to our left. Surely, I think, they've got stories to share. As if sensing my impending intrusion, the men make a break for it, retreating to their pickup trucks as I kick myself for missing my chance.

Shawneen returns moments later with coffee and waters.

"Anything else I can get you guys?" she asks.

"Well," I begin, "I know you're busy but . . ."

I give her the elevator pitch—father and son, retracing the Oregon Trail, rediscovering America, et cetera, et cetera.

Her face brightens.

"Well, if you want to know about the Ranch Hand, then you'll want to talk to my dad. He owns the place. And he should be in any minute now."

Within moments Kale Wuthrich slips behind the counter and is immediately intercepted by his daughter, who introduces us.

"They're retracing the Oregon Trail," she fills him in. "And they want to know about the Ranch Hand."

"Sure," Kale says, turning to us. "What do you want to know?"[2]

Indeed, he is the resident scholar. Kale's career at the Ranch Hand began as a dishwasher in 1991. Twenty-six years later, after filling most of the roles the restaurant had to offer, he became its owner.

"The main reason I bought it," he says, "is so nobody else would."

Kale's protective of the place, as are the thousands of truckers who, since its founding in 1979, have loyally returned to the Ranch Hand while passing through the Bear Lake Valley.

"Our clientele is pretty varied," Kale says. "Lot of tourists, lots of ranchers, and truck drivers from everywhere in the U.S."

"It's a real mixing pot," I say.

"That's it exactly," Kale agrees. "And if you work here, you never grow up to be racist or anything because you see all walks of life. And you learn that we all eat eggs the same."

I smile at the sentiment, one that, admittedly, I hadn't expected to hear over coffee at 8:00 a.m. in small-town Idaho.

"Working here lets you see America in a new way," Kale continues.

"What do you mean?"

He tells me about a time a few years back when thirty Boy Scouts visited the Ranch Hand to retire the establishment's American flag.

"And the minute they started to lower the flag, truckers from every direction pulled up to honor it."

Kale describes how truckers of all ages—"folks who'd just gotten their driver's licenses to folks who'd served in Vietnam"—left their cabs to circle the scouts as they lowered the flag for the last time. Hands on hearts, hats removed, those truckers observed a depth of solemnity rarely seen at the Ranch Hand. Amid pin drop silence, that flag was folded, burned, and retired with all the requisite pomp and ceremony.

No one had planned for such a memorable occasion, but by virtue of its existence the Ranch Hand had ensured that such a wondrously impromptu scene could occur.

"It was a reminder that we're all Americans," Kale says, "even if we live in our separate bubbles."

The truck stop is a gathering place for friends new and old, Kale explains. And some of their clientele will never be forgotten. As proof, he refers us to the memorial pole at the restaurant's entryway, upon which is etched a dozen or so names of valued customers who have since passed on.

One of those names belongs to Kale's grandfather, who, prior to his passing, sidled up to these stools for decades.

"Every day for twenty years," Kale confirms. "We'd sit and have coffee just like you and Henry here."

I get the sense that it's the kind of routine you only fully value in the aftermath. The day that stool is empty, the morning the coffee turns cold.

"Listen guys, it's been great chatting with you," Kale says, "but I better get back to work."

As he leaves, I take a sip of coffee and then turn to my son and smile.

"What?" Henry asks.

"Nothing," I say. "Just making a memory."

★ ★ ★

Henry and I enter Montpelier's National Oregon/California Trail Center just after breakfast. We've barely stepped inside before the forty-four-thousand-square-foot building becomes a bit overwhelming, complete with covered wagon, a gift shop, and executive director Becky Smith greeting us in what appears to be period attire.

"Welcome," Becky says, "you must be the writer."[3]

Becky grabs a few chairs from the lobby near the art gallery, then rustles up the rest of her staff.

"We'll need to involve everybody," Becky explains, as she motions them over, "because it's the team that makes this place happen."

In total there are seven of us: Bob, our wagon master; Diane, a board member and volunteer; Hailey, a staff member; and Hailey's sixteen-year-old son, Hiatt, also on staff. Becky rounds out our circle, with Henry and me seated in the center.

"Well, then," I say, "where to begin?"

Becky gives me the rundown: how from May through September their parking lot is flooded with buses. People come from all over the world, she explains, adding that many visitors see their own lives mirrored in the stories of the emigrants. "And sometimes," Becky continues, "the connections are closer than you'd think."

Becky shares the story of one family who, while visiting the previous summer, became unexpectedly emotional when an audio diary featuring the words of emigrants Margaret and Abigail Scott began blasting from the museum's speakers. The family was visibly shaken, and when a museum employee asked if they were all right, one of the family members explained that they were descendants of the Scotts, whose words they'd just heard.

Not only that, but in the featured diary entry Margaret and Abigail had mentioned that their mother, Anne, was ill. As the family members explained to the museum employee, Anne's bones had recently been exhumed and reburied in Oregon, allowing the emigrant to complete in death the journey she couldn't complete in life.

"That gave us all goose bumps," Becky says.

And it's far from the only example of present-day visitors communing with their emigrant pasts.

"We have people who hang out with us from the past back there," Becky says, nodding toward the interior museum.

People as in . . . ghosts? I wonder.

I've grown so accustomed to talking endlessly about provisions and routes and ruts and swales that this otherworldly topic takes me by surprise.

Becky speaks openly on the subject: describing everything from orbs she's seen in photographs to museum employees' glimpses of a vanishing emigrant women.

"You say to yourself, 'I can't believe it,' and yet . . . I think they understand our struggles," Becky says.

"Struggles?" I ask.

"The pioneers scraped together everything they had to survive, and we do everything we can to survive in our modern world too. I think they sympathize with that, and there are certain things they don't want us to forget."

"Like what?"

"For one, you didn't get to Oregon alone. They were a rolling community," Becky explains, "and they pitched in and helped each other. If old grumpy Gus was being mean, you were kind in return because you didn't know if he'd be the one to hold your hand while you died of cholera."

Fair point.

"They also want us to remember not to give up," Becky continues. "I tell this to young people all the time: don't let anyone dictate your future. If there's something you want to do, you go for it, hell or high water. You might roll your wagon, but you just tip it back over and go on to Oregon. If you want to do something special in your life and people tell you that you can't, do it anyway."

The historical researcher in me wants to dismiss such claims and focus on the proof: the primary sources, the peer-reviewed articles, and the interviews. But the open-minded dreamer in me reminds me to listen. To consider the possibility that there might be lessons to be gleaned beyond the limits of our world.

"Haven't we seen more of this in the last five years?" Becky asks her staff.

Several nod.

"Do you think it's because we need their lessons now more than ever?" I ask.

"That's been my thought," Becky says. "I think they realize that as we progress through time that we're going to need this extra support.

Because we cannot do it alone. No one goes through this life alone. It takes everyone pulling together to make it happen."

I nod, make a note.

"This is a very special place to us," Becky concludes. "And you will never see any ghost hunters in this building. Our people are too special to us."

* * *

Following our time at the museum, Henry and I continue west toward Soda Springs. Had we traveled forty miles to the southwest, instead, we'd have arrived in the city of Preston, the site of the Bear River Massacre—known as the Massacre at Boa Ogoi to the Shoshone people—which holds the horrific distinction of likely being the deadliest (and perhaps least well-known) Native American massacre in history. For years the Shoshone people had resisted the encroachment of emigrants in present-day Idaho's Bear River, though following a series of Shoshone-led attacks in 1862—resulting in the deaths of several miners—the U.S. War Department approved a campaign aimed to quell the "problem."[4]

In the subzero, predawn hours of January 29, 1863, Shoshone chief Sagwitch peered toward a ridgeline above his village to observe what he described as a "cloud" or "steam" or, worst case, "them soldiers they were talking about."[5] His latter guess was the right one.

Materializing out of the fog was the Second Regiment California Volunteer Calvary, led by Col. Patrick Connor. On Connor's command the regiment began their frontal assault, though, after facing strong resistance, took flank positions instead. For four hours the cavalry attacked Shoshone men, women, and children—an attack that became all the more deadly once the Shoshone warriors depleted their ammunition. By morning's end between 250 and 400 Shoshone people lay dead in the blood-stained snow and frozen river.

It is an astonishingly high death count, particularly when placed in context of the better-known massacres wrought against Native Americans, including 1890's Wounded Knee Massacre (approximately 250 Lakota deaths) and 1864's Sand Creek Massacre (between 70 and 500 Cheyenne and Arapaho deaths, the majority women and children).[6] Yet for many Americans, myself included, the Bear River Massacre remains virtually unknown.

It is a footnote to the larger story, just one more massacre alongside the rest.

★ ★ ★

Shortly after passing through Soda Springs I spot a sign that, if it's to be believed, informs me that we are a mere twenty miles from Lava Hot Springs—a "must-see," according to the woman we'd met the previous day at Farson Mercantile.

Though Lava Hot Springs isn't on the itinerary, neither was the storm in Doniphan or the Days Inn in Sidney or the pictographs in the cave with Randy Brown. Some of our best memories were made beyond our preplanned stops, I reason, so why not try for one more?

Because nothing makes the miles go faster than a mystery, I begin floating hints to Henry about our "secret" destination.

"A movie theater?" he guesses.

"Nope."

"A carnival?"

"Not even close."

Twenty minutes later, as we take a sharp left off U.S. 30, the answer reveals itself. Stretched before us is a wonderland of carefully designed hot spring pools and river tubing outfits and a town as quaint as any I've ever seen. The entire place is wedged into a valley along the Portneuf River, the surrounding mountains giving the impression that we've just discovered some unknown, off-the-grid jewel. Of course, nothing could be further from the truth. Though these hot springs were discovered by white explorers over two hundred years ago, the Bannock and Shoshone people had been enjoying them for centuries.

By the twentieth century entrepreneurs understood that there was money to be made in its waters, and today a significant chunk of the town's economy is centered around the springs. We offer our own contribution, forking over fifteen dollars or so for a pair of day passes.

"Now this is the life," I sigh as we ease ourselves into a 102-degree pool surrounded by giant red canopies.

"The life," Henry agrees, his arms spread wide along its concrete edge. But because complaining provides us nearly as much joy as relaxation, we quickly fall back into the grumpy old man routine we'd perfected earlier that morning. Suddenly the water is too hot, the sun is scalding, and where's that gust of wind when we need it? We're tired, we're hungry, we miss our mommies. Still, we make the most of boiling our bodies, and when we emerge from that water, we're as withered as California Raisins.

But we're happy, too, for having had the experience. Kicking our grumpy old men personas to the curb, we remind ourselves of our good fortune. We are alive and together and safe at the bottom of a beautiful valley.

"Man," Henry says as we walk toward the changing room. "I bet the emigrants *loved* coming here."

I eye the vending machines, the gift shop, the outdoor showers.

"How could they not?" I agree.

* * *

Hours later, after concluding a brief stop at Register Rock—an off-the-beaten-path boulder tagged with emigrant names—Henry and I hop back into Bullseye in preparation for the final two-hundred-mile leg to Boise. Yet upon starting the engine, I notice an unfamiliar message scrolling along the Jeep's display screen.

"Well, that's weird," I say.

"What's weird?" Henry asks.

"The screen says, 'Oil Change Recommended.'"

"What's that mean?"

"Well, if forced to wager a guess . . ."

Outside, the brown desert sizzles at a sweat-inducing ninety-one degrees, though inside the vehicle the temperature gauge climbs even higher. I'd insisted on making this stop to impress upon Henry the difficult conditions that the emigrants once had to endure. Though now, with car trouble looming, I worry that lesson's becoming a little too real.

"What do we do?" Henry asks.

"We sit tight," I say, digging around the glove compartment for the owner's manual. "Nothing to worry about yet."

The owner's manual confirms it, noting that the real worrying needn't begin until the "Oil Change Recommended" message changes to the more urgent "Oil Change Required."

Relieved, I place the manual back into the glove compartment. As I do, I spot the business card I'd received from the rental car company back in Eau Claire.

Out of an abundance of caution, I give them a ring.

"How can I help you?" comes the voice on the other end.

I immediately recognize Jake's voice, the jovial rental car attendant who'd helped me the previous Thursday. When I mentioned our trip, he'd seemed thrilled by the prospect. So thrilled, in fact, that he'd thrown in a free upgrade to Bullseye the Jeep Compass—the single, greatest bit of good fortune to befall us the entire journey.

"Jake," I cry with perhaps a tinge too much enthusiasm, "thank goodness it's you! This is B.J."

A moment of silence as he works through his mental Rolodex.

"The guy retracing the Oregon Trail?" I offer.

"B.J.!" he says, his memory jogged. "Wow! How are you guys doing out there?"

"Good! Well . . . pretty good. We're at a place called Register Rock in Idaho."

"Cool!"

"Yeah. But the thing is, we've got this pesky oil change message popping up on the screen . . ."

Jake assures me we'll be fine but that if we'd feel more comfortable getting the oil changed, the rental company will reimburse us.

"But *you* think we'll be all right?" I press.

"I mean . . . *probably* . . ."

Not that we could've done anything about it given our current middle-of-nowhere locale.

At the conclusion of the call, Henry glances up from his composition book.

"What did Jake say?"

"He thinks we'll be all right."

"Oh."

A pause as long as the emptiness stretched before us.

"So . . . we'll be all right," I confirm.

"If you say so."

"I do."

Another pause.

"Dad?"

"Yeah?"

"If everything's fine, then why are we still talking about it?"

Probably because my mind has leaped to the alternative version of events.

Cut to the red-headed vulture soaring over our vehicle, followed by Henry and me dragging our dehydrated bodies through the rattlesnake-infested desert, gasping for water as the sun sinks over the cacti.

Admittedly, we have a few twenty-first-century aces in the hole (namely: a cell phone) to ensure that this particular fate won't come to pass. But when parked in the shadow of Register Rock, all I can think of are the emigrants who tried—and failed—to survive along this very route. Though they didn't have oil changes to worry about, they did have hungry oxen and tired oxen and sick oxen and injured oxen and oxen in need of new shoes. All of which surely fulfilled their worry quota.

Putting Bullseye in drive, I steer past Rock Creek along Register Road until I spot the interstate ahead. I merge into traffic, glancing at the mighty Snake River off to my left. Much like the Platte and the Bear, the Snake River, too, played a vital role in guiding the emigrants westward. The mere sight of it reminds Henry that he's thirsty.

"Dad," he calls, "can I drink from this water bottle?"

"Sure," I say. "Just make sure you screw the cap back on when you're done."

"No problem," he says, indulging in a few generous gulps before sighing mightily.

A minute passes as he fiddles with the cap.

"Dad?" he calls.

"Yeah?"

"I can't get the cap on."

"What do you mean?"

"I mean it won't go on," he says, his frustration growing.

"Now calm down," I say. "Everything's going to be—"

At that moment a new message scrolls across Bullseye's screen: Oil Change *Required.*

"Henry," I say, "I need you to figure it out yourself."

"But Dad—"

"Look, I'm going eighty miles an hour here, and Bullseye apparently requires an oil change. So, I need you to do the one thing that I can't do for you right now. I need you to screw on the cap."

"But I tried . . ."

"Henry," I say, my voice sharpening. "I need you to try again. You're six years old, you're a kindergarten graduate, I know you can do it."

Henry gives it another try, though when he catches me glowering in the rearview, any last vestige of water bottle cap twisting confidence immediately vanishes.

What follows are the longest two minutes of our lives.

"It's not like you're cracking a safe, Henry."

"It just won't go on!"

"It's all about threading! You need to match the threading on the cap to the threading on the bottle—"

"I am!"

"Henry, you survived a storm, remember? And you climbed to the top of Independence Rock! You found Kengstrom in a cave! You ate a single scoop at Farson Merc! You swam in a hot spring! You can do this! Just turn to the left like this," I say, demonstrating a twist with forefinger and thumb.

"That's what I *am* doing!" he wails.

Blame it on the heat, my oil change anxieties, or simply our week of nonstop father-son bonding. Whatever the reason, at last we've reached our breaking point.

"You can do it!" I repeat, louder this time.

"But I can't," he weeps.

This fight has been burbling for months, the result of my frustration with Henry's willingness to throw in the towel whenever things got tough. It started with his shoe-tying struggles ("Can't I just wear Velcro?"), and now it's come to this. Rather than learn a seemingly simple task, he'd tried to outsource the job to me.

In hindsight I probably should've screwed on the damn cap. How easy it would've been to pull to the side of the road, guide him through the careful art of water bottle cap screwing, and then continue on our way.

Instead, I take another approach: screaming at the top of my lungs.

"Henry," I plead, "someday Daddy's not going to be here to do it for you! It's my job to teach you now! Don't you understand? I'm trying to make you self-sufficient! I'm trying to prepare you for this unforgiving, godforsaken world!"

"Wait," he says, his eyes brimming with tears, "when are you not going to be here for me?"

Rather than engage in a candid discussion on the average human life span, I begin a glorious backpedaling.

"Um . . . you know," I soften, "like when you go off to college or . . . whatever."

"Oh," he says. "I thought you were dying or something."

"Let's just focus on the cap for now," I say. "All you have to do is turn it to the left. Please. Show me you can do it."

Summoning a bit of magic we could've used five minutes ago, at last the threads align.

"I did it!" Henry shouts, tears of victory streaming down his face.

"Darn right you did!" I say, pounding the dash.

"The problem was you told me to turn left," he explains, "but I actually had to turn right."

I halt all celebratory dash pounding.

"Huh?"

"You were telling me to turn the cap the wrong direction."

"No bud, I told you turn it this way, to the right," I say, re-creating my demonstration.

"Yeah, but you *said* left."

I realize he may be onto something. But rather than fess up (and lose credibility forever), I do the fatherly thing and lie like a rug.

"I meant *my* right, which is your left."

"But that doesn't make any sense!"

"Think about it," I say (hopeful that he won't), "my left is actually your—"

He convulses with laughter.

"Okay, okay," I say, trying a new tact. "How about this: it was all a test. I was testing you so that you could learn another valuable lesson."

"Don't drink water?" he guesses.

"Never—under any circumstances—listen to your father."

In the time it takes most people to screw on a water bottle cap, our lowest moment becomes our highest. Henry cackles at my stupidity.

"Listen, pal," I say, shooting a grin in the rearview, "just remember that I'm the guy who plucked burrs off your butt this morning."

Since it beats crying, we laugh until the road runs out. We leave the dust behind, the ghosts behind, and make this mile a memory too.

29. Henry's illustration of Zoo Boise. Courtesy of the author.

8 Small Kindnesses

Oh, I feel so lonesome today. Sometimes I can govern myself, but not always, but I hold in pretty well considering all things. Trying to write walking but it won't do. We stopped for the night in a pretty place.

—Agnes Scott, 1853

THURSDAY, JUNE 14

WEATHER: PERFECT

RATIONS: SUBMARINE SANDWICHES, DENNY'S RESTAURANT

BOISE ID → BOISE ID

We wake in Boise to spot an animal no westward traveling American emigrant ever saw: an African lion.

"Do you think she looks hungry?" I whisper to Henry. "Because she looks pretty hungry to me."

Henry grins, then waves to her from his place behind the glass at Zoo Boise.

"Hi lion," he says. "Thanks for not eating me."

At last we are engaged in what might be considered a conventional vacation activity, and Henry's reveling in it. Throughout the morning we wander the zoo's many promenades, marveling at the sloth bear, the giant anteaters, and the herd of snuffing capybaras, the latter of which, a sign informs us, are the world's largest rodents.

"And I thought the mouse in our kitchen was big," Henry says.

But of all the animals we'll see that day, none compare to the mighty butterflies, hundreds of which flap throughout the butterfly house just past the Animals of Asia exhibition.

To diminish the chance of butterfly breakout, prior to entering, Henry and I are corralled through two sets of secure doors. Upon entering the first, we're welcomed by a "butterfly wrangler," a fellow whose commitment to the safety of both butterflies and humans is admirable, if not a little funny.

"If a butterfly lands on you and you are uncomfortable for *any* reason—any reason at all—then someone in a blue shirt will help you remove it," the butterfly wrangler says.

Though I have several follow-up questions ("How many ways can a butterfly make a person feel uncomfortable?"), I bite my tongue to ensure that the butterfly wrangler can faithfully enact all protocols and safety measures.

When at last we're granted access to the butterfly house, we enter a wing-filled wonderland. Dozens, if not hundreds, of butterflies float from branch to limb to flower. Their wings appear thinner than cheesecloth and are festooned with designs far lovelier than any mortal hand might make. That such a gentle creature might also seem so regal is as bewildering as it is awe-inspiring. To hell with the lions; I'll take butterflies any day.

So will Henry, by the looks of things. He makes himself a statue among the foliage, ever hopeful that some brave butterfly might grace him with its presence. I become a statue alongside him, hopeful for my own close encounter. As we wait, I reflect on how far we've come as well as how far we still have to go. A week ago at this moment, Henry was squirming in his kindergarten classroom, his eyes boring into the clock. Meanwhile, I'd been doing my own squirming—double-checking checklists, repacking bags, and watching online videos on the proper way to use a snakebite kit. That we are now doing our best perch impressions in a butterfly house in Boise is as unexpected a turn as I can imagine. Unexpected because on some level a part of me never believed we'd make it this far. It wasn't the ruggedness of the road I feared but my own lack of ruggedness. I figured that somewhere along the way we'd face some hardship—a torn tent, a flat tire, a sprained ankle—that would prompt me to raise the white flag.

We'd given it a good faith effort, I'd reason, U-turning toward home. *No shame in turning tail.*

Yet as I stand statuesque in that butterfly house, I realize that not even a team of well-shod oxen could drag me away from our intended destination. Not anymore. We have logged the miles, put in the time, and won't quit until we reach the Willamette Valley. For lack of a less clichéd phrase, this trip has become personal: a test of mettle and verve.

A few feet ahead of me, Henry attempts to pass his own test. Stone-faced, his eyes scan toward the banded king shoemaker to his left. The shoemaker flirts, tiling its antennae toward him as if preparing for landing, and then, at the last second, swoops off to anoint another. Henry sighs; he hasn't been this downtrodden since the previous day's water bottle calamity. Still, he remains optimistic, redirecting his eyes toward a couple of monarchs whom he hopes might think better of him.

Ultimately, it's not the shoemaker or the monarchs that gives Henry a shot but the giant owl butterfly, whose bark-colored wings open and close like a heartbeat. As it drifts closer, Henry shouts without shouting, releasing the loudest whisper I've ever heard: "Da-ad!"

"I know, I see it too."

The giant owl hovers an inch above his head before descending to his shoulder blade. Henry cranes his neck halfway around, *Exorcist* style, in an attempt to catch a glimpse.

"She's right there," I assure him. "She's just sitting there."

It is a kindness Henry can hardly fathom. Of all the kids in the butterfly house, she chose him. Henry bows humbly, his eyes closed as he tries to feel her feelers on his back. It is a consecration, a baptism by butterfly, and when it is over—once that great owl flutters to the next child—Henry seems somehow older, wiser, a boy who can now boast of his brief fling with a butterfly. As we exit through the first set of doors, the butterfly wrangler asks us to turn around to ensure that no butterflies have attempted to "hitch a ride." We endure our visual body scan before getting the all clear from the butterfly wrangler.

"You two have a nice day," he says, opening the door wide for us.

"Thanks for your work," I tell him.

I mean it.

* * *

We don't break any axles, we don't lose any wheels, but by midafternoon it's clear that Bullseye's in need of attention. We'd barely left the zoo before the "Oil Change Required" message continues its chiding. My anxiety rises, though rather than deal with the problem, I do what comes naturally: block it altogether from my mind. After a week on the road, I want to give Henry what he's more than earned: one carefree day *off* the road. And preferably out of a mechanic's shop.

For the next couple of hours we hole up in the Boise Library, not only because it's free and air-conditioned but because it's barely a block from the zoo. If Bullseye has any intention of dying on us, then I prefer he do so within walking distance of the two most kid-friendly places in the city. Upon entering the library, Henry zips toward the kids' section. Before I can catch up, he's already enrolled himself in the summer reading program.

"Think we can finish the whole thing today?" he asks, staring at the program's guidelines.

For the next two hours we read our way through one book after another; books about fairies and goblins and monsters and trolls—pretty much books on every subject other than the Oregon Trail. We make short work of the summer reading program, collect our prize, and then stride triumphantly toward the library bookstore—our best bet for leaving with a book of our own given our lack of library cards.

As Henry examines the picture books, my eyes fall to a collection of poems by Ruth Whitman titled *Tamsen Donner: A Woman's Journey*. I flip the book wide to find poem after poem written in the voice of Tamsen Donner—the ill-fated emigrant who lost everything (including her life) while en route to California in the summer and fall of 1846 and the brutal winter months that followed.

There's no easy way to tell Tamsen Donner's story. Or the story of the Donner-Reed party generally. Over the years the name *Donner* has become synonymous with the horrors of cannibalism, when in fact, their story—much like the story of the West—is far more complex. Yet for simplicity's sake, history often boils their tale down to its tragic end. One that's all the more tragic given the hopefulness with which they'd embarked upon their journey. Even two and a half months in, the members of the Donner-Reed wagon train retained great optimism. Virginia Reed, just thirteen at the time, recalled how on July 31, 1846, "without a suspicion of impending disaster, we set out with high spirits on the Hastings Cut-off."[1]

Which was a big mistake.

The so-called cutoff was alleged to shorten their trip by three hundred miles, when in fact, the thick foliage made passage all but impossible. Prior to taking the cutoff, the Donner-Reed party had averaged a respectable twelve miles a day, though as a result of it, their average soon dwindled to two miles a day. The party pressed through the underbrush as best it could, though hacking through miles of unforgiving terrain soon took its toll. Even deadlier than exhaustion were the lost days the wagon train incurred as a result of the cutoff—time they could hardly spare if they hoped to reach California before winter. Adding to their trouble was the impenetrable heat, dwindling provisions, lost cattle, a broken axle, declining morale, and the earliest snowfall in the Sierra Nevada in decades.

Realizing that mountain travel had become impossible, by mid-November the majority of the party settled in a makeshift camp near Truckee Lake on the eastern side of the Sierra Nevada. By then the wagon train had grown to eighty-one members, the result of several families and individuals who'd joined up along the way. Yet as the Breens, Kesebergs, Murphys, Eddys, Graves, and Reeds prepared their cabins near Truckee Lake, the Donners—unable to catch up with the others—were forced to construct their own camp six miles to the east, at Alder Creek.

As food grew scarce, new sources of sustenance emerged: animal hides, boiled bones, freshly slaughtered family dogs. One day oxen became most useful as food, and so they, too, were killed.

Human flesh was simply the natural progression.

Throughout the ordeal small kindnesses were attempted, though as the situation turned dire, even offerings of bread and blankets became more than most families could spare. For many in the Donner-Reed party, Christmas morning of 1846 was just another dismal day alongside the rest. But thanks to the careful planning of Margaret Reed, on that morning her children were treated to something remarkable.

Hidden within in a pile of snow was a smorgasbord of delights: dried apples, beans, bacon, and fish. Moreover, Margaret encouraged her children to eat as much as they liked. Years later Patty Reed, just eight years old that winter, recounted the scene. "So bitter was the misery relieved by that one bright day," Patty reflected, "that I have never since sat down to a Christmas dinner without my thoughts going back to Donner Lake."[2]

While many well-documented examples of human goodness sprung forth from the tragedy, even today we can't seem to shake the more lurid details of their story. Our macabre fascination in cannibalism is undeniable, though I'm most interested in how their plight speaks to larger themes related to manifest destiny and, by extension, the American Dream itself. Hadn't these emigrants—by way of their hard work and stick-to-itiveness—done everything that was asked of them? Why, then, had they encountered such doom?

Not only were these emigrants' efforts unrewarded, but they were punished for them. How were prospective overland travelers supposed to square that circle? As details of their deaths emerged, so, too, did a less-enticing narrative.

Sometimes the West provided opportunities beyond one's wildest dreams, other times only horrors beyond those dreams.

★ ★ ★

Because we splurged on the all-day zoo passes, we return there late in the day. This time we come bearing our library bookstore purchases (*Mad Libs* for Henry, *Tamsen Donner* for me) and take up residence at a picnic table opposite the giraffes. It is a far different backdrop than the one the Reed family faced at Truckee Lake. Yet they, too, found comfort in literature. Since they couldn't eat the books, they read them, Virginia

Reed noting the many "pleasant hours" spent rereading *The Life of Daniel Boone* while trapped in their cabin beneath a blanket of snow.[3]

Eliza Donner, though not yet three years old, recalled her mother, Tamsen, recounting "wondrous tales of 'Joseph in Egypt,' of 'Daniel in the lion's den,' of 'Elijah healing the widow's son,'" among other inspiring stories.[4]

As Henry loses himself in *Mad Libs* ("Dad, is *fart* a verb?"), I lose myself in Ruth Whitman's reimagining of the life and death of Tamsen Donner. In writing her poems in Tamsen Donner's voice, Whitman attempts to re-create the emigrant woman's lost journal—an artifact that historians have long sought. Whitman's re-creation of the journal, filtered through a poetic lens, invites readers into Tamsen Donner's interior world. But in reading the poems, I revel mostly in the exterior world, paying closest attention to the mention of places where Henry and I have visited: Fort Laramie, the Platte River, Independence Rock. That Tamsen Donner and the rest of the train were once there too—with no knowledge of the tragedy soon to befall them—is in itself rather tragic. From my place in the present I want to shout to the past: "Turn back, Tamsen! Turn your family around and return to Illinois!"

But hindsight is of little use to the dead.

No doubt about it, yesterday matters—just not as much as today.

★ ★ ★

Since the "Oil Change Required" message shows no signs of leaving, we drive to a Jiffy Lube a mile or so from downtown Boise. Freshly reminded of the perils of the Donner party, I'm no longer comfortable taking risks. We pull Bullseye into an open parking spot, then walk into the waiting area.

"How can we help you?" asks the young oil-specked technician.

I explain the situation. He nods, asks for the keys, and offers to take a look.

Henry and I wander the waiting area, which is as forgettable as every waiting area on earth: white-walled, nondescript, complete with a painting print or two.

Within minutes the technician returns with inconclusive news.

"Well, the oil's dirty all right," he says, "but it's sort of right on the line."

"So, if it was you . . . ," I press.

"If it was me," the technician says, sucking air through his teeth, "well . . . how many miles you got left?"

"We're going to the coast. So around five hundred."

"I'd probably ride it out," the young technician says. "But then again . . ."

In walks a man in a blue Jiffy Lube shirt. His name's Dave, according to his stitched name tag. Various pens spill out of Dave's breast pocket, while atop his head rests a hat balancing shades.

"Did you tell him?" Dave asks.[5]

The young technician nods.

"And it's a rental?" Dave asks, directing the question to me.

"Well, yeah," I agree, "but I already called the rental agency, and they promised they'd reimburse me for the—"

"They're not gonna reimburse you," Dave says confidently. "Or if they do, it's gonna take months."

"Well, even if they don't," I continue, "I don't mind paying out of pocket. What's an oil change? Like thirty dollars?"

"Not on this car," Dave says. "The synthetic mix will run you sixty dollars, minimum."

I do the math: that's two nights in a KOA, twelve Little Caesars pizzas, a couple tanks of gas.

Then again, it's a small price to pay for peace of mind.

Do the right thing, I think. *Don't be a cheapskate for once.*

"Like I said," the young technician continues, "if it was my car, I'd probably keep going."

Dave waves him off, then leans in close.

"Listen," he says, "I'm not gonna have you and your son getting stranded in the desert somewhere." He turns toward the technician, asks for the keys, and then wanders away.

"So . . . what's happening?" Henry whispers as we take our seats in the waiting area.

"I have no idea."

Dave returns ten minutes later, handing me the keys.

"We topped 'er off," he said. "It'll get you there."

Though I'm not sure I know what "topped 'er off" means, I understand the last part.

"Thanks, Dave. I appreciate it."

"No problem," he says. "Where you two headed again?"

"The Oregon Trail!" Henry shouts.

"We're retracing it," I explain.

"No kidding!" Dave laughs, his eyes widening. "Well I'll be . . ."

"How much do we owe you?"

"Nothing," he says.

"Well, at least for the oil . . ."

"Nah."

"But . . ."

"Nope."

"Can we send you a postcard?" I ask, desperate to offer him something. "I mean, it won't keep the lights on, but—"

"A postcard sounds good," Dave agrees. "Safe travels."

Henry and I walk back toward Bullseye, dazed by Dave's kindness.

"So . . . he fixed it?" Henry asks.

"Apparently."

"And he didn't want money?"

"Apparently not."

Henry buckles into the back seat, then readjusts his hat.

"That's one nice stranger, huh?" he says.

"He's no stranger," I say. "That's Dave."

★ ★ ★

In 1852—while in the throes of grieving for her recently departed mother—eighteen-year-old Margaret Windsor stumbled upon a baby along the trail who'd apparently lost its own parents. As the story goes, Margaret took responsibility for the child, faithfully carrying it for the next five hundred miles and inquiring at each campground whether any nursing mothers might offer the child sustenance. Margaret's request was never refused.

Oregon Trail tales are replete with similar acts of kindness, including one featuring Eliza Donner herself. Shortly after her rescue from Truckee Lake, three-year-old Eliza and her surviving sisters were transported to Sutter's Fort. The girls were malnourished and in need of food, and their hero came in an unlikely form: a red-haired boy not much older than them. According to Eliza, the boy told her to meet him near a cow pen, and when she did, he handed her a tin cup overflowing with fresh milk. "You needn't say nothing to nobody about it," the boy told her.[6] "I gave your little sister some last time and I want to do the same for you. I hain't got no mother neither, and I know how it is."

Eliza accepted the milk and drank deeply, never forgetting the boy or her debt.

★ ★ ★

That night, shortly before bed, Henry and I lean against our motel balcony and peer up at the sky. We're within spitting range of the Boise Airport, and the constant flow of planes keeps us occupied for a good half an hour or so. Ahead of us, we see a world quite different than the one we've grown accustomed to. To our left: a Denny's sign. To our right: an endless stream of cars.

The momentary change of scenery suits us fine. Over the past week what once seemed like modest luxuries (hot coffee, dry towels, a copy of *USA Today*) now seem like riches beyond our wildest dreams. Still, I miss the babble of Montpelier Creek, the moonglow of Douglas, even the sound of the wind-rippled tent at the KOA near Casper. Don't get me wrong—we'll take the queen beds and the ice machine; we just don't need them anymore.

The longer we watch those planes, the more I marvel at our world. Though far from perfect, I like to think it steers toward kindness. That there are more folks like Dave than not. And more folks willing to share a cup of milk rather than drink themselves to excess.

"Hey Dad," Henry says, "remember that butterfly that landed on me?"

"I do," I say.

"That was awesome."

"Our whole day's been awesome."

After another plane lands and another moment of introspection, Henry continues. "You know," he says, "we should try for another awesome day tomorrow."

"I'll put it on the itinerary," I say.

30. Henry's illustration of Ann Kiser's grave. Courtesy of the author.

9 The House Always Wins

When the last Red Man shall have perished, and the memory of my tribe shall have become a myth among the White Man, these shores will swarm with the invisible dead of my tribe, and when your children's children think themselves alone in the field, the store, the shop, upon the highway, or in the silence of the pathless woods, they will not be alone.

—Chief Seattle, 1854 or 1855

FRIDAY, JUNE 15

WEATHER: A BEAUTIFUL 78 DEGREES; SKIES STRETCH FOREVER

RATIONS: MORE PEANUT BUTTER SANDWICHES

BOISE ID → BAKER CITY OR → PENDLETON OR

Here's what doesn't happen: we don't break down in the desert, our wheel well full of snakes. Nor do we become stricken with cholera or shoot off our toes with our pistols. We don't take the wrong route and become trapped in a mountain pass. We don't run out of food. In fact, barring a storm and the need to "top off" the tank with clean oil, our trip has proceeded mostly as planned. We rolled the dice and didn't lose, which in my estimation is a win.

We've been driving less than an hour on Interstate 84 when my eyes spot a sign off the highway.

"Oregon!" I shout. "We're in Oregon!"

Though I've been anticipating this sign for two thousand–plus miles, it still takes me by surprise.

Henry peeks up from his composition book to find me pointing toward the WELCOME TO OREGON sign.

"Can you believe it?" I shout.

"Yes!" Henry says. "I can!"

We pull off at the Oregon Welcome Center, putting Bullseye in park and running toward the giant wooden marker. We take our positions: me brandishing my Joker grin, while Henry stands alongside me, his left hand to his left knee as he peers out at the world with an explorer's gaze.

"On three," I say, doing my best to work the newfangled selfie-stick. "One, two . . . oh crap, I dropped it. Let's try this again. One, two . . ."

After several failed attempts—most of which feature nothing but the top half of my head—we at last snap a good one.

"We did it!" Henry says. "We made it to Oregon!"

And then the anticlimax sets in.

"So . . . now what?" he asks.

We don't have a cabin to build or land to till or gold in need of panning. Somehow, in all those months of preparations, it never occurred to me what we might do upon arriving at our destination.

In truth we haven't technically arrived at our destination. We're in Oregon, sure, but we've still got a few hundred miles before reaching the Willamette Valley, the endpoint for many of the overland emigrants. Still, we're almost there, which means, too, that our trip is nearly complete.

Somewhere on the horizon, I see the flicker of a finish line. I wish it were farther away.

* * *

Forty or so miles north of the welcome center, we enter a stretch of highway so deep into a valley that all we see above us are hills. Hills that, to a couple of midwesterners, look an awful lot like the Alps. Somewhere beyond their peaks we catch a sliver of sky—a thin ribbon of blue lining the tops of the trees.

31. Welcome to Oregon, Ontario, Oregon. Courtesy of the author.

My knuckles whiten as we drive into those hills. The Snake River rushes off to our right, though I don't dare lift my eyes from the road to admire it.

"We're driving straight into them!" I holler.

"Watch out!" Henry calls, playing along.

It feels like I'm steering the front car of a rollercoaster, my heart climbing in my throat as I guide us up and down and around those twisted turns.

"These mountains are *huge*!" Henry calls, his hands suction-cupped to the window. "But . . . but I still feel like I can hold them!"

I smile. What better way to describe the strangeness of scale in this landscape? Of feeling both big and small, safe and vulnerable, powerful and powerless too.

"Hold on tight," I cry. "Here comes a big drop!"

He lifts his hands, closes his eyes, and together we begin our descent.

★ ★ ★

An hour beyond those hills, somewhere off state highway 86, we spot a sign for the National Historic Oregon Trail Interpretive Center. At first the sign seems like a bluff—*You're telling me there's a museum out here?*—but we're right to call that bluff. On a hilltop high above us rests twelve thousand square feet of museum, each of which, we'll soon learn, is jam-packed with replica wagons, taxidermied bison, and dioramas and exhibitions as far as the eye can see.

By this point in the trip Henry's interest in museums rivals his interest in swales. Still, anything beats another hour buckled into Bullseye. He exits the vehicle in high spirits, jogging toward the museum's front entrance.

Inside, we're welcomed by a clean-shaven young park ranger, who loads us down with twice our weight in pamphlets. When I make the mistake of mentioning that I'm writing a book, he loads us down with more.

"Oh, and don't forget these," the ranger adds, tossing in a couple kid-themed activity books.

"This is all great," I grunt, shifting the materials' weight in my hands. "But while we're here, I'm wondering if we might speak to someone directly? Someone with knowledge of this portion of the trail? Not that these pamphlets aren't great," I'm sure to add.

"Let me put in a call to the museum's director," the ranger says.

Moments later I'm shaking hands with Sarah Lecompte and thanking her for her time.[1]

"It's my pleasure," she says. "This is a pretty special place."

It's special for a lot of reasons, she explains, though most of all for reminding visitors like Henry and me that we humans have long been in motion.

"The Oregon Trail is an especially well-documented migration," Sarah says, "but it's just one more example of what's happened throughout the human experience."

Moving is what we do and what we have done for millennia. Though humans migrate for any number of reasons, most migrations boil down to a single motive: we leave a place in search of a better place. It's as true today as it was thirty thousand years ago, when humans first crossed the Bering Land Bridge, likely in search of food and a better climate.[2] Such migrations are never easy and never without their risks. Still, humans have taken these risks again and again, and if the past is any indication of the future, this pattern will continue.

Though Baker City played but a minor role in the Oregon Trail story, the city still overwhelmingly supported the construction of the interpretive center due to its potential economic impact.

"I imagine the museum's brought in a lot of visitors?" I ask.

"Over two million," Sarah confirms—nearly fivefold the total number of westward traveling emigrants from that era. "It's really kind of bizarre," she laughs, "but it's true."

Bizarre, sure, but also the result of good marketing.

"The Oregon Trail is sort of an iconic cultural identifier for people in this state," Sarah says, and Baker City didn't want to miss out.

While the museum has, indeed, made its economic mark on the region, for Sarah—like so many park rangers, site directors, and historians I've met—the preservation of history remains the primary objective. For her there's nothing more meaningful than helping museumgoers find personal connections with their past, including genealogical links.

While I, too, had hoped to uncover some genealogical link to the emigrants, so far my efforts have fallen short. Much to my disappointment, both my paternal and maternal ancestors were content making Indiana their finish line.

Would it have killed them to go farther west? I've long wondered.

(The answer, of course, is maybe.)

Shortly after saying goodbye to Sarah and beginning our tour of the interpretive center, I serendipitously stumble upon a link: not a genealogical one but a geographic one. Etched onto a replica gravestone ahead of us, I read the following:

In Memory of
Ann Kiser
Wife of Daniel Kiser
Of Fort Wayne
Allen Co., In.
Who Died
August 26, 1852

The names mean nothing to me, but the place means everything:
Fort Wayne, Indiana, is my hometown.

"Henry! You won't believe this."

By now he's fully engaged in a museum scavenger hunt ("Where
the heck is that taxidermied rattlesnake?"), though he halts his hunt
to examine the gravestone.

"So?" he says.

"Look where she was from," I say.

"Fo . . . rt Way . . . ne?" he reads.

"That's where Grandma and Grandpa live. That's where I grew up!"

"Oh," he says, "did you know her?"

"Buddy, how old do you think I am?"

"Maybe . . . a million?"

"Why don't you keep looking for that rattlesnake," I say irritably.
"I hope you find it."

As he searches for the rattler, I begin my search for information
on Ann Kiser. Reaching for my phone, I type Ann's name, death date,
and location into a search engine. Yet even with the full power of
the internet at my disposal, I don't learn much other than that Ann
died at the age of twenty-five.

Later I'll fill in a few more blanks thanks to emigrant Henry Allyn,
who in 1853 traveled from Fulton County, Illinois, to Oregon's Willamette Valley and left behind a journal. His entry from July 26 mentions
Ann Kiser, or rather, Ann Kiser's skull, which a fellow emigrant discovered as they pitched their tents near Salmon Falls Creek in Idaho.[3]

"Soon after we discovered a grave on an eminence not far from
the spring that had been dug open and a number of bones scattered

around it," Henry recorded. The following day's entry offers greater detail: "We collected all the bones we could find and together with the skull and whatever fragments of grave clothes were scattered around and the pillow which was under the head of the corpse and put them into the grave and covered them up as well as we could. We had nothing but a small fire shovel to work with. There was a board at the head of the grave on which was carved 'In memory of Ann Kiser.'"[4]

Which solves the mystery of how he knew to whom the skull belonged.

But there's another mystery: why did Henry Allyn even bother mentioning Ann Kiser's name? Death had become commonplace by that point in the trail; why make note of some stranger?

Yet in doing so, he offers me the link I've been looking for. Is it possible Ann and I once roamed the same Fort Wayne riverbank? Might our feet have graced the same ground? We only missed each other by 132 years—a blink by some measures.

Though much of Ann's life and death remains unknown, I'd wager wolves were to blame for her disinterment. Henry Allyn righted that wrong, taking it upon himself to rebury the woman he never knew. Aside from sharing the earth, Henry and Ann shared no earthly connection. But in her death he found the opportunity to connect on a human level. It didn't matter that he didn't know her personally. What mattered was that he understood the golden rule of the trail: do unto others as you'd have them do unto you.

After all, under different circumstances it might've been Henry Allyn's skull beside the spring that day. In which case some other traveler would've been tasked with reaching for the shovel.

And hopefully, jotting a name in a journal too.

★ ★ ★

Turning off the highway near Pendleton, Oregon, our eyes lock onto a towering structure vaulted upward to the sky.

"What is that?" Henry asks, pressing his nose to the window.

"Wildhorse Resort and Casino," I say, reading the sign.

"What's a resort and casino?"

"Like Chuck E. Cheese," I explain. "But for adults."

"Can we go?"

"Maybe later," I say. "First we're headed to Tamástslikt Cultural Institute."

"Is it another museum?" he asks worriedly.

"Of course not," I say. "It's a cultural institute."

"So . . . a museum?" he clarifies.

"Trust me," I say, "this one's different."

While the museums we've previously visited had all shared portions of the Native American story, Tamástslikt promises the most in-depth perspective, specializing in the regional history of the Cayuse, Umatilla, and Walla Walla tribes. It's just what we in need: a richer, deeper, and Native-centered perspective on the American West.

Stepping from the car, we find ourselves on the Umatilla Indian Reservation.

"Where's everyone else?" Henry asks, glancing at the cultural center's mostly empty lot.

"From the looks of things," I say, nodding to the packed parking lot in the distance, "I'd say everyone's at the casino."

Stepping inside Tamástslikt, we're greeted at the information desk by sixty-year-old John Bevis, an elder from the Umatilla tribe.[5]

"What can I do for ya?" he asks, adjusting his wire-rimmed glasses.

"Two tickets, please."

"Oh, he's all right," John smiles, nodding to Henry and charging me for one.

I tell him about our journey, our project, and in particular, how we hope to learn more about westward expansion's impact on the culture of America's indigenous people.

"Well, our museum should be pretty helpful then," John says. "We try to give a perspective you don't always find in the other museums."

When I ask John what most visitors fail to understand about westward expansion, he doesn't hesitate.

"For one, in the beginning it was amicable, and things were going okay," John says. "I guess it was good for about forty years, maybe. But toward the end, it started to get ugly."

Most historians agree. Prior to the never-ending flood of emigrants, Native Americans and white travelers regularly and productively engaged in what one historian described as "trade and aid."[6]

New to the land and its many dangers, emigrants regularly called upon Native Americans for support. And for the right price, many were willing to oblige. One area in which emigrants found themselves particularly inept were river crossings. On numerous occasions emigrants foolhardy enough to attempt such crossings unaided ended up losing livestock and, on occasion, their lives. No river was more dangerous than the Columbia, though if the emigrants had managed to make it that far, they likely had the good sense to hire Native American guides to see them across safely. One guidebook from the era remarked that the river "requires the most dexterous management, which these wild navigators are masters of, to pass the dreadful chasm to safety. A single stroke amiss, would be inevitable destruction."[7]

Native Americans were compensated for their trouble (clothing and ammunition were both highly sought), and for a time the arrangement appeared to be mutually beneficial. Trade, coupled with what some might describe as mutual respect, managed to keep the peace—at least for a time. But it didn't take long for some emigrants and Native Americans to begin viewing one another in a less favorable light. So unfavorable that not even trade could mend the truce that had been broken.

"What changed?" I ask John, knowing full well that one of the major changes had to do with the droves of invading emigrants populating Native lands. But John surprises me with a different answer, one I'd never even considered.

"Well," John says, "what you were getting then were the grandchildren of the Indian fighters back east. So now they're migrating west, and they've heard all these stories that Grandpa told them about fighting Indians."

"So, this later wave of emigrants was going off of stories they'd heard from their grandparents about eastern Indians?" I clarify.

"They figured we were all the same. I've heard stories of our people being sniped for no reason other than being Indian," John reports. "I always wondered how the heck they got the wagons through the mountains. That should have given us a window to measure the perseverance of these people that we'd be dealing with in the future. And," he adds, "the aggressiveness they'd bring with them."

Indeed, if emigrants were willing to risk their lives for the potential of a better life, there was no telling how far they'd go to ensure their success—even at the expense of others.

"The problems really started when they came right through our backyard," John continues, referring to the Umatilla lands upon which we're standing. "Our neighbors, the Yakima and the Nez Percers, they kind of got bypassed, but they came right through our backyard, so we kind of felt the brunt of the expansion and the manifest destiny. We were dealing with them on a daily basis."

And not all those interactions were positive.

Still, for many Native Americans, the occasional "passing through" of emigrants on tribal lands—though far from ideal—rarely spurred violence. The problem was the emigrants who stuck around: claiming land, exploiting resources, and making themselves at home in another's home.

The trickle of emigrants soon became a flood, prompting many Native Americans to more fully realize the wide-reaching extent of the problem.

"If the Great Father kept white men out of my country," remarked Red Cloud, chief of the Oglala Lakotas, "peace would last forever."[8] But by 1867 time for such talk had passed. Keeping white men off Native Americans' land was, for the U.S. government, out of the question.

Despite such intrusions and exploitative measures, according to John, for the Umatilla people, aside from occasional instances of violence, "it balanced out, the good and the bad."

"Really?" I ask, more than a little surprised.

"In the beginning the Indians messed around with them too."
John smiles.

"What do you mean?"

"I've heard stories about mock war parties. Especially from here down to The Dalles," John says. "They would go and chase off all the livestock and then let the migrants go out and look for them, give them a day or two maybe, and then send a young boy in who says, 'I can help you find your animals for a nominal fee.' Of course, the Indians would be holding their animals just three or four miles away. They'd let them go a couple more days and do it again."

Though the grift hardly makes up for the destruction of Native lands, community, and culture, John wants me to understand that his ancestors fought back, often employing brains rather than brawn, as evidenced by the "missing livestock" ruse.

"And your ancestors—your great-great-grandparents—they were in the middle of all this?"

"Could have been," John says.

"Did you ever hear any personal stories about how your family was impacted by emigrants?"

"No, not really," John says. "Grandma and them never really talked about it. Our neighbors, the Nez Perce, they can go all the way back, and they've got the names of people and all of that. But we're kind of weak in that area."

One reason why, John explains, is because the Umatilla people were taught to embrace humility.

"When these events happened, we didn't really talk about it much. So it kind of got lost. We remember major events, but the names . . . those have kind of been lost in a way."

John turns toward the clock, his shoulder-length silver hair draped behind him.

"It's my lunch break now," he says. "But we can talk more after lunch, if you like."

I thank him, we shake hands, and then Henry and I start toward the cultural institute's long stretch of exhibitions. We study pictures and placards on a number of subjects—from the Cayuse, Umatilla, and Walla Walla tribespeople's agricultural and hunting practices to craft making and the oral tradition. We learn about the importance of horses, the influx of disease as a result of emigrant travel, and the United States' many attempts to assimilate Native people—destroying centuries' worth of culture in the process.

Here there is no mention of brave emigrants "taming" the frontier. No mention, either, of rugged cowboys who ruled by way of lasso and six-shooter. At Tamástslikt there is no place for such whitewashed history. What we learn, instead, is the history of a people whose lives were upended as a result of the emigrants' intrusion into the West.

Prior to visiting, we'd had some sense of the exploitative actions that occurred at the hands of the emigrants, though by the end of our visit we'd come to know that story far more acutely. In particular, the U.S. government's role: a death by a thousand cuts strategy including the 1830 Indiana Relocation Act, the Dawes Act of 1887, and plenty more legislation to come. The former resulted in the displacement of no fewer than 100,000 Indians, many of whom endured the forced march that became known as the Trail of Tears. Four thousand Cherokees died en route. It was a tragedy on every level. But upon stepping back further, the death count spurred by the Trail of Tears is comparably small given that between 1500 and 1900 the population of Native Americans declined from 12 million to approximately 237,000. Disease was the primary killer, responsible for 90 percent of the deaths. Not only was the encroachment of white Europeans to blame, but in some instances their disease spreading was by design. In a letter written in 1763, Sir Jeffrey Amherst, commander in chief of British forces in North America, advised Col. Henry Bouquet at Fort Pitt of one particularly horrific strategy to "deal" with America's indigenous people: "You will do well to try to inoculate the Indians [with smallpox] by means of blankets, as well as to try every other method, that can serve to extirpate this execrable race."[9]

Whether the spread of disease was intentional or not, it had its effect. The calculus is difficult to compute, especially when the number we use most often only accounts for deaths. But how many families were separated as a result of U.S. Indian policy? And how much culture was decimated in its wake? We have a hard time quantifying the full impact because there are no agreed upon measures to do so. If it were a natural disaster like an earthquake, we might rely upon a Richter scale. But the death and destruction inflicted upon Native people by white Europeans is anything but natural.

As Henry and I wander the exhibitions at Tamástslikt, I am continually astounded by all that I don't know.

Is my ignorance innocent, I wonder, *or is it willful?*

★ ★ ★

A year after meeting John Bevis at Tamástslikt Cultural Institute, we speak again, this time by phone, and this time with no six-year-old listening.[10] When I ask John for a few more details on his Umatilla heritage, he chuckles.

"Shit, I had to fight for that."

"What do you mean?"

"I'm what you'd call a half-breed," he says.

His father—a white man whom John refers to as a "teepee creeper"—impregnated his Umatilla mother and then abandoned the family nineteen days after his birth.

"So, growing up was kind of like a curse," John continues. "You're not wanted in either world. The Indians are always trying to test your so-called Indianness, and the white guys don't want you either." It wasn't until John left high school—and got a closer look at 1960s civil rights turmoil—that he began to fully embrace his Umatilla heritage. By the late 1960s John became engaged with many of the ideas set forth by the American Indian Movement (AIM)—from poverty to police brutality to the preservation of cultural identity. Though he was hardly a leader of the AIM movement, he was a careful listener, a thoughtful learner, and an occasional rally participant. But in later years he became disillusioned by the Red Power movement.

"In the beginning I wholeheartedly supported [the American Indian Movement]. But as I got older and saw what they were doing, it kind of lost its flavor."

John was particularly unsupportive of AIM's 1973 occupation of Wounded Knee, a demonstration that involved hostage taking and firing on federal officials, leading to the deaths of two Native activists. None of this sat well with John, who faulted the demonstrators for negotiating rather than maintaining their stand—to the death, if necessary—as many had promised. But he doesn't blame the demonstrators exclusively. Equally responsible, John says, was the Federal Bureau of Investigation, whose alleged infiltration of the demonstrators ultimately led to the protest's less-than-satisfying end.

"The best way to handle your AIM problem was to have your implants there with a case of beer," John explains. "That was a known fact at some of these rallies." The FBI's alleged approach to handling the Wounded Knee Incident—set alongside the backdrop of the Vietnam War—led John to conclude that "the government has a dark side and its own agenda."

When I ask John about the greatest problem facing Native Americans today, he doesn't hesitate—non-Native people's ignorance of Native culture.

White people's understanding of indigenous people is so limited—and so reliant on unflattering and unfounded stereotypes—that it's difficult for white people to view Native Americans as equals, John explains.

"Just take this past weekend," he says.

While driving home from a powwow, John passed several police cars near White Swan, Washington. Curious by such a strong display of law enforcement, upon returning home, he searched the internet to find the cause of the trouble. An online article revealed the horrific truth: that five Indians on the Yakima Indian Reservation had been murdered shortly before he'd passed by.

After reading the article, John made the mistake of scanning readers' comments.

"All of it was pure negative," he says. "It was terrible, nasty." After scrolling through 150 or so disparaging remarks on Native Americans, John thought to himself, *And they have the nerve to act surprised when we say white people are racist?*

"White racists are busy calling everyone else racists," John tells me. "The Muslims, Mexicans, all of that. They're calling them names, but how come the white man can never admit [that they're racists too]?"

John pauses as he lets this sink in.

"That's his Achilles' heel," he says. "He [the white man] can never admit it. If he would just be honest with himself and say, 'Yes, we did do all of this and we want to make it better,' but instead, they just kick dirt in your face."

If white people want to make a sincere effort toward righting a few wrongs, John says, they might start by fighting against the appropriation of Native symbols, particularly in sports mascots.

"If you want to stop something, stop the tomahawk chop bullshit you see in the stadiums," John says, his voice rising. "'Oh, we're just having fun,' they say. Fun to you but at the expense of other people."

John takes a breath, regains composure.

"When I give tours here at the museum, I do an introduction on how it's not a blame game. How the [cultural institute] isn't to make you feel bad, just to show you that in the beginning, we were different but that we all learned to come together as Americans. But guess what?" he continues. "*We* were America's firstborn."

Yet the "who was here first" argument mattered little to the white politicians who crafted America's eighteenth- and nineteenth-century Indian policies. By hook or by crook the U.S. government swindled and stole all that it could in every cowardly and dishonorable way imaginable. Dee Brown's classic text *Bury My Heart at Wounded Knee* recounts this in full, sparing no detail of the horrors wrought upon America's indigenous people by the white people who came after. I'm embarrassed to admit that I was thirty-five by the time I read Brown's book. Perhaps I was afraid of what I'd find within its pages. For decades I'd shrouded myself in ignorance, overlooking the gut-wrenching specifics of the systematic slaughter of Native people. That I *could* look away is one of the most egregious examples of my own white privilege. It's not enough that I've been personally spared every reverberation of such horror; I couldn't even bear the truth of the transgressions.

"What can white people do today?" I ask.

"Find out [the truth] for themselves," John says. "Don't believe everything you see in the movies and read in the books. That's what our interpretive centers and museums are all about. Some of it's generic, sure, but you might just come across a guy like me who will fill in the gaps."

As our conversation nears its end, John tells me that setting the historical record straight begins with education. Collectively, we must all be willing to take an unflinching look at our country's darkest chapters. And to listen, too, for the lyrics we don't hear in songs like "America the Beautiful." We must think critically, engage our curiosity, and settle for nothing less than a sustained study of difficult facts.

"But that's the trouble with America," John sighs. "We dumb it down."

★ ★ ★

Upon leaving the cultural institute, Henry insists we make a stop at the casino.

"Why?" I ask. "You feeling lucky?"

He is not. Neither of us are. What we feel is numb. Embarrassed. And more than a little ashamed by our emigrant ancestors. Henry tries taking comfort in the knowledge that we—by which he means he and I—didn't directly cause the mass slaughter of indigenous people. Yet as I explain to him, we are nonetheless the direct beneficiaries of such actions.

"What do you mean?" he asks.

"Well," I try, "every day we live in our skin, and because of its color, we experience the world with privileges that others don't have."

"Like what?"

"Well," I begin, "like when you watch TV, for instance. Chances are you always see people who look like us."

He nods.

"Now imagine how it might feel if you didn't see anyone who looked like you."

He nods again.

"Superman's white, Batman's white, Mr. Incredible's white. Wouldn't it be better if people who don't have white skin could turn on their TVs and see more people who looked like them?"

He keeps nodding.

Ahead of us a dozen white folks stroll toward the Umatilla reservation's casino. They walk the world with the same impunity that I do, fearing little, except, perhaps, losing their shirts in a hand of cards. I want to redirect them to Tamástslikt Cultural Institute, but before I can, the doors swing wide and slot machines' songs spill forth: *Ding-ding-ding-ding-ding-ding-ding!*

After some pleading from Henry, I agree to a quick peek inside the casino, hopeful that Oregon's gambling laws will ensure that my son keeps his own shirt.

We've barely entered through the automatic doors before my worst fears comes to fruition: the Wildhorse Resort and Casino is a wonderland. We are overwhelmed by the onslaught of lights, sounds, and a seafood buffet as wide and deep as the ocean. It's so far removed from what we've grown accustomed to (campgrounds and peanut butter sandwiches) that we hardly know how to respond. Since Henry's too young to step foot on the casino floor, we loiter near the entrance, which happens to be connected to a movie theater featuring the latest Pixar film.

"Oh man," Henry says, his eyes locked on the movie poster, "oh man oh man—"

"Come on," I say. "We just saw a movie four nights ago in Casper!"

"Wait—that was only four nights ago?" he asks, breaking his gaze from the poster.

"I know," I agree. "It feels like a year ago, huh?"

"More like two years."

I steer him away from the movie theater, only to turn a corner to find a fully staffed kids' area, complete with ball pits, child-sized hamster tubes, and a shelf overflowing with video games—the kid's version of hitting the jackpot.

"Just when I thought it couldn't get any better . . . ," Henry whispers.

"Keep it moving," I say, leading him toward the door.

"Dad," he says as I drag him away, "I think I really like casinos."

"You don't," I assure him. "You like Chuck E. Cheese."

32. Henry's illustration of Portland, Oregon. Courtesy of the author.

10 Redrawing the Boundaries

When I was born, thirty miles of railroad comprised the whole mile-age of the United States, and this only a tramway. Now, how many hundred thousand miles I know not, but many miles over the two hundred thousand mark. When I crossed the great states of Illinois and Iowa on my way to Oregon in 1852 not a mile of railroad had been built in either state.

—Ezra Meeker, 1907

SATURDAY, JUNE 16

WEATHER: 77 DEGREES

RATIONS: DONUTS

PENDLETON OR → PORTLAND OR

The following morning I wake to nature's alarm clock: a sparrow perched on a nearby fence. He's relentless in his chirping, and so I drag myself from my sleeping bag and crack wide Ruth Whitman's *Tamsen Donner: A Woman's Journey*. I've barely owned the collection for a day, but already, I've reached the book's final poem, "Where Is the West," which begins: "If my boundary stops here / I have daughters to draw new maps on the world."[1]

I have a son and a daughter with the potential to do the same: to clear a path and trod a trail and continue on when my own life reaches its own boundary. It's a thought as comforting as it is macabre, the poetical take on the harsh reality that none of us are getting out of here alive. And it's a reminder, too, that this dawn in Pendleton—complete with this breath of fresh air and that darn chirping sparrow—isn't some detour to a future moment but in fact, the moment we've been waiting for. Road trips make it easy to forget this simple lesson. When you're only peering into the distance, you overlook the road beneath your wheels.

Admittedly, this is a lot to take in, pre-coffee. Since I can't pin this particular existential crisis to that sparrow on the fence, I blame it on the previous night's fitful sleep. No sooner had I closed my eyes than I'd been visited by a series of ghosts à la *A Christmas Carol*. Not the ghosts of past, present, and future—though thematically, that would have been quite helpful—but only the ghosts of the past.

Enter Ann Kiser, formerly of Fort Wayne, who stirred a pot of beans over our fire. Next came Tamsen Donner, who anxiously awaited a bowl of Ann's beans. Then came the children: Henry Dyer, Mary Hurley, and Joel Hembree, all of whom lounged in the grass near our tent, wide smiles brimming across their faces. I wish I remembered more details from the dream, but I wake with only the foggiest recollection. By the time the sparrow rouses me, our campsite is back to belonging solely to Henry and me. There's no ash in the firepit, no empty bowl of beans, no child-sized indentations in the grass.

An hour or so later, Henry stirs, stumbling from the tent and walking barefoot toward me.

"Hey, buddy," I say, "did the sparrow wake you?"

"Why can't birds ever sleep in?" he asks.

"Well," I say, "it's sort of their job not—"

"Yeah, yeah, yeah," Henry says, reaching for his *Mad Libs* and pen. "Hey Dad," he says, "give me a verb."

Regardless of the part of speech, my answer is almost always *fart*.

Ten minutes later, after the "smelly" (adjective) "orangutan" (noun) has "farted" (verb) on top of the "Ferris wheel" (noun), we're packed and ready to go. We turn left out of the KOA, but no matter how fast I drive, I can't leave behind the memory of those ghosts. There they are, plucked from my dream and scrunched into the back seat alongside Henry.

After all these miles and all these days, we've inadvertently created our own wagon train.

I keep the ghosts close. A reminder that my boundary, for the moment, continues.

★ ★ ★

Somewhere along I-84 West, I spot a sign for the Bridge of the Gods.

First opened in 1926, for ninety-two years the steel truss cantilever bridge has faithfully connected drivers between Cascade Locks, Oregon, and Skamania County, Washington. The bridge's name demands our full attention, though admittedly, bibliophile that I am, I'm most inclined to stop due to its prominent role in Cheryl Strayed's 2012 best-selling memoir, *Wild*. It's the bridge where Strayed concludes her 1,100-mile solo hike of the Pacific Crest Trail, a journey inspired in the aftermath of death and divorce, amid other personal problems.

Since our own journey is fast approaching its end, it seems only fitting that we, too, pay our respects to the bridge. Shortly after entering the town of Cascade Locks, we wind up the hill toward the toll road that grants access to the bridge. But we wind too far up the hill and soon find ourselves in the toll lane. Since I don't mean to cross into Washington, I pull off into a "personnel only" lot. Momentarily free from the stream of traffic, I take the opportunity to stretch my legs and snap a quick picture of the bridge. But the woman working the toll booth is having none of it.

"Can't park there!" she hollers.

"I know," I say. "I'm sorry. I'll snap a picture and be on my—"

"Can't park there," she repeats, louder this time.

"Right. I'll only be a—"

"Can't," she growls, "park—"

"All right!" I shout, stomping toward Bullseye. "I'm leaving, okay?"

I open the car door and slam it louder than necessary.

"What was her problem?" Henry asks as I re-buckle.

I want to tell him that sometimes people are jerks. Which is true.

But after two deep breaths and ten seconds of reflection, it occurs to me that I'm the one being the jerk. Had I obeyed the sign, we could've avoided this unpleasantness altogether.

The problem, though, is that this trip has spoiled us. Over the past two thousand miles, Henry and I have grown so accustomed to unexpected kindnesses that anything less than a red carpet and a ten-gun salute suddenly feels like a personal affront.

"I'm the one who screwed up," I tell Henry, putting Bullseye in reverse. "I'm the one who didn't obey the sign."

"But you were only there for like . . . a second!" he says.

"Yeah, well, it was still a second too long."

Out of loyalty to me, Henry shoots that toll worker his grumpiest glower.

"Hey," I say as we wind down the hill, "don't be like that. It's good to be good at your job. And that's all that woman was doing."

"But now we'll never get a picture of the Bridge of the Gods," he complains.

Down the hill I spot a restaurant parking lot with plenty of empty spaces. Since no signs turn us away, I pull into one with a picture-perfect view of the bridge.

"Looks like we might get that picture after all," I say.

Conjuring the full power of his sourpuss face, Henry grumbles that it'll have to do.

It's not that he's upset, I realize, but ashamed.

Of me.

I'd made a mistake and admitted it.

It would've been easier to spin the story so that the toll worker took the blame. I'd have saved some face and a little credibility in the eyes of my son. Short-term credibility, at least. But now Ruth Whitman's got me thinking long term of life's boundaries and of the maps Henry will one day draw without me.

"Where should I stand?" Henry asks.

"Um . . . maybe over there?"

33. Bridge of the Gods, Cascade Locks, Oregon. Courtesy of the author.

We sink low at the edge of the parking lot as I position the camera before us.

"Smi-le," I call.

For posterity's sake we do.

Even if it kills us, we are committed to making every damned mile a memory.

"Did we learn a lesson back there?" I ask as we veer back onto the interstate.

Henry isn't listening; his attention is fully focused on the composition book on his lap.

"Well *I* learned a lesson," I say in the off chance he's listening.

Ahead of us I see no red carpet, no ten-gun salute.

Just road and road and road.

* * *

We've barely entered Portland, but I'm already desperate to leave. It's not Portland's fault. Who doesn't love a city whose most popular slogan is "Keep Portland Weird"? The problem is that Portland *is* a city, and cities are what we've been trying to escape.

But there's no escaping Oregon's largest city as well as the place where the Willamette and Columbia Rivers converge. It was a much quieter place in the 1850s, when the town's 821 residents had run of the place. Today the population's swelled to well over 630,000 residents, each of whom seems to have made it their personal mission to clog the freeway ahead of us.[2]

The West's transition from territories to booming cities is a story that extends beyond Portland's borders. In later years, when emigrant Ezra Meeker reflected on the once small town of Puyallup, Washington—which he'd helped found in 1877—he described a place greatly at odds with the rural landscape he'd known: "Instead of the slow, trudging ox team, driven to the market town sixteen miles distant, with a day in camp on the way, I see fifty-four railroad trains a day thundering through the town. I see electric lines with crowded cars carrying passengers to tide water and to that rising city of Tacoma . . . I see a quarter of a million people within a radius of thirty miles, where solitude reigned supreme for fifty-four years ago, save the song of the Indians, the thump of his canoe paddle, or the din of his gambling revels."[3]

Much like Puyallup, by the early 1900s Portland, too, had dramatically changed, its natural splendor irrevocably altered by human interference. While trapped in traffic on I-84, it's easy to lament the transformation, though for late-nineteenth-century emigrants the burgeoning metropolis surely seemed like proof of manifest destiny's claims. In 1845 journalist John O'Sullivan had proclaimed it America's destiny "to overspread and to possess the whole of the continent," and fifty years later that so-called destiny appeared to have been fulfilled, particularly in places like Portland.[4] Though perhaps "destiny" had less to do with it than the usual motives—arable land, access to waterways, and the opportunity for financial gain.

"Are we there yet?" Henry calls.

"Does this look like a bookstore to you?"

After a cursory glance he agrees that the bumper-to-bumper freeway in no way resembles the bookstore where I'm scheduled to read later that day.

Admittedly, were it not for the reading, we might've kept on driving. But since it's bad form to blow off one's reading, we continue our crawl, arriving at the bookstore half an hour before showtime.

I'd been told it was customary to bring beer, and so Henry and I head to the nearest gas station to pick up an eighteen-pack of Henry Weinhard's. When we return to the bookstore, I note that we are the only ones there.

Probably could've gone with a six-pack, I think.

Thankfully, my Seattle-based aunt, uncle, and cousin fill a few seats, as do a pair of bookstore employees who take pity on me. At final count, in a city with well over half a million residents, a whopping one member of Portland's general public is in attendance. Frankly, I've had worse turnouts. On the upside Liz, the woman in attendance on her own volition, has enough enthusiasm to fill the room.

"Oh, Henry," Liz gushes, "I bet you and your dad are just having the greatest time, huh?"[5]

"I guess . . . ," Henry says.

"These memories will last a lifetime."

"Maybe," he agrees.

While reviewing my notes in the moments preceding the reading, I glance up from my pages to spot Henry and Liz chatting merrily in the back of the store. She's holding Henry's hallowed composition book—the one he's kept hidden from me since striking out. With Henry's blessing she begins scribbling upon its pages. Moments later he begins walking her through the many sketches he hasn't yet shared with me.

Am I frustrated by the snub? Maybe a little. But I don't have time to make my frustration known. Since I don't want to disappoint my relatives, the bookstore employees, and Henry's new best friend, Liz, I begin my presentation, regaling the "crowd" with our less-than-harrowing tales from the trail.

"The past nine days," I begin, "have been the best nine days of my life."

But for the forty-five minutes that follow, I struggle to explain why. How could I ever describe the magic we'd found within those miles? Instead, I prattle on about storms and springs and forts and rocks and sunbaked peanut butter sandwiches. About caves and ruts and swales. And mosquitos. And butterflies. And the Bridge of the Gods. But none of it comes close to conjuring the heart-thrumming buzz that's been welling within me. No words come close to replicating the experience. It seems a disservice even to try.

To spare myself the giant hook, I cut my talk short and thank everyone (by which I mean Liz) for coming.

"I just loved hearing about your trip," Liz tells us at the reading's conclusion. "And if it's okay with you, Dad," she continues, reaching into her purse, "I'd like to give Henry this."

She offers me a five-dollar bill.

"Oh, we can't accept—"

"Please," she says, thrusting the crinkled bill into my palm. "I don't have grandchildren. Just take it. Let him buy a souvenir at the next stop."

"Yeah, Dad," Henry says, coming to Liz's defense. "Let me buy a souvenir at the next stop."

Because I am outnumbered, I relent.

"Well . . . it's very kind of you," I tell her. "And don't worry. I'll make sure he doesn't blow it all on candy."

"Oh, he can spend it anyway he likes," she says, moving toward the door. "I'm just glad to be a part of your trip. Goodbye, Henry."

"Bye," he calls to her. "Thanks again."

As Liz leaves, I turn toward Henry.

"What were you two gabbing about back there anyway?"

"Dad," he whines, clutching his composition book to his chest, "a little privacy?"

★ ★ ★

That night we trade in the campground for floor space at my friend Ellie's house.[6] Ellie, her partner, and their dog, JD, welcome us heartily, keeping us company as we unfurl our sleeping bags along their living room floor.

We stay up much too late, Henry mesmerized by the grand return of a TV screen, while Ellie and I talk about the trip. I share with her the many kindnesses we've been the beneficiaries of, the abundance of goodwill that always somehow steers our way. From the hat-snagging woman in the storm to Dave the Mechanic to Bookstore Liz and her gift of the five-dollar bill.

"It's as if people can't wait to help us along," I say. "Honestly, I'm a bit baffled by it. How quickly all those strangers became friends."

"That's awesome," Ellie says. "It really is. But . . . I wonder how your trip might've been different if you weren't a straight white guy with a six-year-old."

Ellie's words halt me faster than a busted axle.

"I mean, I'm really glad you guys are having a great time and all," she adds. "I'm just saying . . ."

It's a lesson a long time in the making, though one I'd failed to see through its proper lens.

"You're right," I say. "You're absolutely right."

And there it is: the truth.

In trying to "rediscover" America, I'd missed most of it. So focused on the geography beyond the window, I'd overlooked my geography within. I'd become so transfixed by the myths of the emigrants that I'd paid too little attention to the horrors they wrought in their wake. And of equal importance: how those horrors have reverberated into the present.

How easy it is to forget our place in history. And how easy it is to look elsewhere when we can. That white Americans like me have long exploited our way to our "exceptionalism" isn't merely a historical fact but a current event.

Had Henry channel-surfed through the news that night, he would've found plenty of proof of this in the stories. Including the previous day's acknowledgment by the Department of Homeland Security that some two thousand immigrant children had been separated from their families during border crossings between April and May.

Had he turned on the news a week earlier—on the day we'd endured Doniphan's storm—he would've witnessed exploitation of a different sort: coverage of oil now flowing through the Dakota Access pipeline, despite protests from the Lakota and Dakota people, whose sacred lands we'd co-opted yet again.

How to explain white privilege to a six-year-old?

Though we'd discussed it hypothetically in the aftermath of our visit to the Tamástslikt Cultural Institute, I'd failed to apply it to our trip. Ham-handedly, I'd referenced Superman and Batman and Mr. Incredible, when I should have been talking about us.

I should have told Henry that his skin is a shield to hide behind but that he mustn't hide behind it. And explained that shields can be weapons, too, when other people don't possess such protections. I should have told him that every mile of our lives is a chance to find a different path. And that the near constant unfurling of the red carpet that we'd received wasn't necessarily a reflection of the generosity of America but the generosity of America toward people like us.

That night, as Henry and I snuggle deep into our sleeping bags, I think back to Ruth Whitman's words: "If my boundary stops here / I have daughters to draw new maps on the world."

But what maps will our children choose to draw? And what boundaries will they dare break?

For hours the moon bathes my sleeping boy's body in light.

I remain awake, unsettled.

34. Henry's somewhat accurate illustration of giving me his Father's Day gift. Courtesy of the author.

11 The Gift

We arrived . . . at Oregon City, situated at the Falls of the Willamette, the place of our destination. This was the 13th of November, 1843, and it was five months and nineteen days after we left Independence, in Missouri. Here we were able to procure such things as were really necessary to make us comfortable . . . and were happy, after a long and tedious tour, over mountains and deserts, through a wild and savage wilderness, to witness . . . the home of Civilization.

—Overton Johnson and W. H. Winter, 1843

```
SUNDAY, JUNE 17—FATHER'S DAY
WEATHER: 77 DEGREES
RATIONS: FRUIT AND YOGURT PARFAITS
PORTLAND OR → OREGON CITY OR → NEHALEM OR
```

I wake to the Oregon sun slipping through the windows. Rubbing my eyes, I struggle to find my bearings.

Where's the campground? The tent? The firepit?

Instead, I'm forced to make do with running water, a flushing toilet, a shower, and a towel on a rack.

And coffee. Glorious, freshly ground coffee.

Crouched on the living room floor, I spread my map before me. All signs point to a good day ahead of us: just a twenty-mile jaunt from Portland to Oregon City, then another hundred miles to our last stop of the trip, Nehalem Bay State Park.

That we've reached the last leg of our journey seems somehow impossible. The undertaking that we'd dreamed for months has entered its final phrase. Two more sleeps and we'll be back in our beds in Wisconsin.

Henry stirs to the sound of my map folding.

"Morning!"

He leans on one arm, stares at me squinty-eyed, and then—with an enthusiasm I've rarely seen from him at such an hour—shouts: "Dad! We need to get to Bullseye!"

"Huh?"

"Come on!" he says, leaping to his feet. "Let's move!"

Reaching for my keys, I chase after him. Prancing barefoot through the gravel drive, I unlock the Jeep, then watch as he crawls into the back seat. He paws through his backpack, tossing aside toys and markers and candy wrappers until he finds what he's looking for: his top-secret black-and-white composition book.

He thrusts it into my palms.

"Here," he says. "I made you a book."

"Wait . . . what?"

"Here," he says again. "This is for you."

Holding it in my hands, the reality sinks in.

"You . . . made me a book," I say.

"Yup!"

"How long have you been working on it?"

"Umm . . . maybe the entire trip?"

I steady myself.

"You mean you've been dreaming this up in the back seat the whole time and you never told me?"

"Yes, because it's for Father's Day," he says. "It's for you."

I flip through dozens of monster-filled pages, at which point he directs me to the end of the story.

"Somebody helped me on the last page," he explains.

"Who?"

"The woman in the bookstore."

My mind flashes to the previous night's reading, when Henry and Liz had hatched their beautiful plan.

Scrawled in a handwriting that is not my son's, I read his message aloud.

"'Dad,'" I begin, a golf ball forming in my throat, "'I like when you draw a big world with me. I like when you take me out and we go and do stuff together. I like when you write books.'"

My eyes close, then open.

"Oh, buddy," I whisper.

"And look," Henry continues, "there's a hidden picture right there."

I nod, reveling in every sketch and scrawl he's made for me. But it's the opening line of his message that I can't shake.

I like when you draw a big world with me.

How to tell him that he's the reason I draw it at all?

"Hey," I say, reaching for his shoulders, "look at me for a sec."

"What?"

"I love this book."

"I know."

"It's the best thing ever."

"Yeah," he agrees, "those monsters were really hard to draw."

"All this time I thought I was the one writing a book about our trip and yet . . . you wrote it."

He shrugs.

"Promise me we'll fill this whole book with adventures."

Sure, he agrees. Why not?

★ ★ ★

If there is an official "end" to the Oregon Trail, then Oregon City is as good a spot as any. Today it's home to the eponymously named End of the Oregon Trail Interpretive Center, which we'll visit within a few hours' time. But first Henry and I are committed to celebrating Father's Day by eating the best fast-food breakfast Oregon City has to offer. We take our tray outside to enjoy the outdoor seating overlooking the Willamette River. It's a nice enough view, though no match for the Pacific Ocean, which we'll see upon our arrival in Nehalem later in the afternoon.

"And we can swim in the ocean, right?" Henry asks.

"Sure," I say, "if it's not too cold."

Our conversation's interrupted by a grumbling man in a pickup truck off to our right. He's waiting for his order, and when the fast-food employee—a Latino man a few years my junior—hustles over to deliver it to him, the employee's met with a tirade of four-letter words.

They are so vile, and so uncalled for, that for a moment I am stunned into submission. I literally cannot move—not to cover Henry's ears or to intervene on behalf of the employee. By the time I find my feet, the driver has found his truck's accelerator—screeching off into the distance.

Henry can't avert his eyes, now glossed with tears. He has never seen anything like it and, for the life of him, can't understand why the man in the truck was so angry. Because he had to wait for his hash brown? Because a hash brown is worth as much as human dignity? Because diminishing a person over something so small is a way to make another person feel big?

I am two seconds too late to do much of anything. Still, I rise and walk toward the employee. My hands shake, and my face burns, though I rein in my emotions as I speak to him.

"I'm sorry that happened to you," I say. "He . . . he had no right—"

The employee lifts an eyebrow, as if unclear about what I'm referring to.

"That man," I say. "In the truck—"

"Oh that?" the employee says. "That's nothing. It happens all the time."

Within moments he's back to taking the next order while I'm left wondering what it's like to face that "all the time."

"Didn't that truck driver know it's Father's Day?" Henry asks.

"Yeah, man," I sigh. "I guess not."

★ ★ ★

Oregon City's earliest settlers were often far more welcoming. Rather than curse one another, they sought out ways to assist. In 1845, upon learning of the Barlow-Palmer party's attempt to construct a road across the Cascade Mountains (providing travelers a much-needed alternative to the dangers of floating down the Columbia River), Oregon City citizens gave generously to the cause. One historian noted that "approximately 1,100 pounds of flour, 100-pound of sugar, and smaller portions of coffee and tea" were offered in support, in addition to local citizens providing pack horses and other forms of relief.[1]

Such generosity toward emigrants extended outward, much of it coming from an unexpected source: John McLoughlin, the French Canadian chief factor of the British-owned Hudson Bay Company. The influx of newly arrived emigrants into the region was a direct threat to British interests, yet despite the company's orders *not* to assist the American emigrants, McLoughlin did otherwise, regularly extending assistance in the form of food, clothing, lodging, and medicine. In further defiance to his British employer, in 1844 McLoughlin "extended over $31,000 of company credit to approximately 400 needy settlers." This in addition to McLoughlin employing his personal wealth toward the same goodwill gestures.[2]

There were other unexpected acts of generosity too. One historian described a circus in Portland that held a "benefit performance" for emigrants, raising three thousand dollars in the process. And of a steamboat company that "transported relief supplies" to needy travelers free of charge.[3] People helped in the ways they were able and, in doing so, eased the suffering of those who came after.

While raising funds and donating supplies were both important shows of support, the most impactful way to assist emigrants with their most pressing needs was to form relief parties, many of which consisted of volunteers who, having survived the journey themselves, were aware of how far a little help might go toward ensuring fellow travelers' success. Nothing made this clearer than the gut-wrenching aftermath of the Donner party. In response, the number of relief parties grew. It was difficult work, though lives were saved because of it. And for imperiled emigrants no sight was a greater gift than a well-supplied relief party on the horizon.

It's such a simple idea: to extend a hand when a hand is needed. Yet how often we do otherwise.

★ ★ ★

Following our eventful breakfast on the Willamette River, Henry and I buy tickets for the End of the Oregon Trail Interpretive Center.

Well, at least I buy Henry a ticket.

Fathers, the ticket seller informs me, are free today.

Once inside, we introduce ourselves to historian John Jarvie.[4]

"You're the guys retracing the trail!" John smiles. "Welcome to the end of it." Decked out in a brown vest atop a green-and-white checkered shirt, John resembles an overland emigrant himself—his dark hair and salt-and-pepper beard only adding to the facade. Leading us outside, we stand beneath a giant map of the trail, one nearly identical to the map at the National Frontier Trail Museum in Independence. Back then the trail ahead had seemed so perilous. But now, having endured it, it just seems like something we did.

"Well," John says, turning to Henry, "what's been your favorite placc?"

"Um . . . ," Henry says, stalling as his eyes scan east to west.

"How about this?" John asks, pointing to Independence Rock.

"We climbed that," Henry says, then lowers his voice to a whisper, "even though we weren't supposed to."

"I'm not sure we weren't supposed to," I say. "It . . . just sort of seemed that way."

John laughs.

"Have you done the trail too?" I ask.

"Nah. I've only done west of Independence Rock," he says. "I haven't seen Courthouse Rock, Chimney Rock, any of that."

"It's worth seeing," I say with the confidence of a man who knows.

"What was *your* favorite spot?" John asks, turning the question to me.

Taking a step back from the giant map, I list the obvious places: Scotts Bluff, Guernsey Ruts, Chimney Rock, Fort Laramie, Independence Rock. But the more honest answer is that my favorite

35. End of the Oregon Trail Interpretive Center, Oregon City, Oregon. Courtesy of the author.

spots are the ones you won't find on this map. They're the places we nearly missed: Lava Hot Springs, Farson Mercantile, the Ranch Hand Trail Stop. It's the mini golf course in Douglas and the playground in Bar Nunn. It's the movie theater in Casper. Yet to admit that I prefer the kitsch to the natural splendor risks jeopardizing our trip's central premise. After all, this journey was supposed to be about history! And rediscovery! Of course, all that "history" and "rediscovery" isn't worth too much if you're not living the lessons today.

As John and I talk, Henry turns his attention to a patch of nearby trees. I watch from a distance as the boy who once wouldn't leave my side now swings from a low-hanging limb. As our conversation winds down, I ask John the same question I've asked everyone.

What can we learn from the emigrants?

"Well," John begins, "maybe we can learn something from their toughness. I mean, it's just amazing to me. So many of them packed their saddlebags with water and provisions and headed out into the unknown. And many of them knew nothing about this interior region of the country. It's just so foreign to our way of thinking today," he says. "When I go on a trip today, I have to know every last detail: where I'm staying, where the electricity is coming from, the running water. And to make matters more difficult, these folks were bringing along their wives and children—"

"With no guarantee of anything," I say.

"That's right," he agrees. "There was nothing waiting for them."

"Was it worth it?" I ask.

"You know," John says, "I sometimes think about how the emigrants could've stayed home all along. How they could've developed good relationships with their family and friends and had a great experience right there in their home communities. I mean, that's what I would have done." He pauses before continuing. "Then again, so many were quite successful in the West. I guess it comes down to your idea of contentment versus the desire for more. As an individual today, I just think: 'Be content with what you have.' But that wasn't them. And I suppose that's what made us a nation."

If faced with that choice myself—especially under nineteenth-century conditions—I, like John, would've sought contentment right where I was. Leave the adventures to the adventurers and the risks to the risk-takers. If my family and I had food in our bellies, a roof over our heads, and enjoyed the liberties due to us all, then I'd have never dared venture west.

What might Henry have done? I wonder.

A dozen yards away I watch as he crouches, turning his attention to the grass. Who knows what he sees—a grasshopper, a toad, maybe a praying mantis? All I know is that he appears to be enjoying himself fully.

One mile at a time—and one moment at a time—he's drawing his own big world.

★ ★ ★

Though the map is technically correct in noting that we only have one hundred miles to go, it fails to mention that the last twenty miles down U.S. 53 is a hairpin-turning, stomach-churning test of my driving skills. The single-lane road cuts through Oregon's towering trees, darkening and brightening the world in equal measure. Some moments the canopy doesn't allow for so much as a beam of sunlight; other times the rays all but blind me.

Henry and I fill the time with jokes I'd memorized from his joke book.

"What did the big bucket say to the little bucket?" I ask.

"What?"

"You look a little pail!"

He cackles.

"What kind of flowers are on your face?"

"What kind?"

"Two-lips!"

He howls.

"Why did the cookie go to the hospital?"

"Why?"

"He was feeling crummy!"

The miles pass like seasons, but the jokes help carry us through. When at last Henry's had as many miles as he can handle, Bullseye, rather mercifully, approaches the gate to Nehalem Bay State Park.

A few months earlier I'd monopolized a good fifteen minutes of a park employee's time with dozens of questions about campsites: which was closest to the bathroom, the playground, the beach. Eventually, we'd decided on site D29, and as we park the car onto the accompanying patch of pavement, it's clear that phone call paid off. With the exception of the windswept plains just outside of Casper, every campsite has exceeded our expectation. But in Nehalem Bay the world really outdoes itself.

The beach beckons, but since I now possess the discipline I'd previously lacked (read: I recognize the value of tent stakes), I insist we first set up camp.

"But the ocean—" Henry moans.

I give him my "You'll-thank-me-if-the-monsoon-strikes" look.

Together we make quick work of it, trading in our Laurel and Hardy tent-raising shtick for our best impression of two people with some knowledge of camping. Which, at this point in our journey, is a fair assessment. Henry, who on day 1 couldn't tell a ground tarp from a rainfly, now knows the purpose of every last strap in the tent bag. We move with a newfound fluency, transforming our grassy plot into a complete campsite (including hammock!) within minutes.

After shimmying into our swimsuits, we head toward the narrow path leading to the beach. We can't see the water, but we can hear it, the waves growing louder as we approach. Henry can restrain himself no longer. His feet slip in the sand as he climbs toward the top of the dune.

Upon reaching its crest, he spots the Oregon coast heaving below. Henry, who hasn't seen the ocean since he was a baby, trembles at the sight of it. I can't keep him from bounding down the dune, and why should I? The driftwood doesn't slow him nor the shells or the seaweed. Once his feet catch traction on the wet sand, he only increases in speed. He hurls himself into the water, screaming—part joy, part glee, part biological response to a warm body being plunged into a cold one.

I stop just short of the water, my feet sinking a quarter-inch into the sand.

"How is it?" I ask.

"Freezing!"

He runs parallel to the water until exhaustion sets in. Then he collapses, rather dramatically, face first into the sand.

That afternoon we trudge along the beach for miles. Through it all the landscape never changes—the shoreline stretching on like an infinity mirror. Our walk back is just as enjoyable, the distant, tree-lined cliff serving as the only physical marker we've got. Yet even with it, we still manage to get a bit lost. All that sameness proves disorienting, and as we search for the trail back to our campsite, we overshoot it by a quarter-mile. No matter. Our only punishment is a longer walk on the beach.

We return to our campsite just long enough to replenish supplies: refilling our water bottles and packing our picnic dinner. But as Henry and I dig through our food bag, we notice our provisions have dwindled.

"Pretty slim pickings," I admit, pushing past a couple granola bars only to find a couple more.

"Is this it?" Henry asks, reaching for a pack of cracker crumbs.

"Well, we've always got more peanut butter and bread if you—"

"No," Henry says. "No more peanut butter sandwiches."

We opt for the only non–peanut butter sandwich option at our disposal: a gelatin cup, a pudding cup, a sports drink.

"Won't find this on any menu," I say as we take our place atop a dune in full view of the ocean.

By 6:oo p.m. the beach is all but deserted. That so much beauty is shared by so few seems somehow wrong. I don't recall what we talk about. All I remember is folding into the routine that we'd perfected, basking in our quiet ease. When the pudding runs out, we take turns leaping down the dunes, marking our places in the sand like a couple of long jumpers. And then, an hour later, when the day runs out, we turn our backs to the water.

At the campsite we gather soap, towels, and toothbrushes, then start toward the shower house. Even in twilight, the campground is overrun with Frisbees and bikers and dogs. With laughter and barking. The sound of a squeaky swing—which comes by way of the playground adjacent to the shower house. A young child, maybe two, squeals as his father sends him soaring.

The boy babbles, and the father asks: "Higher? You want me to push you higher?"

The boy confirms it with more babble.

Towels draped over our shoulders, Henry and I watch the pair.

"You know," I say, "that was us not too long ago."

Silence.

"Henry?"

I turn to find I'm suddenly alone.

Just inside the shower house, I hear the water clatter.

One foot in front of the other, I follow.

★ ★ ★

"Dad?" Henry asks as we extinguish the fire.

"Yeah, bud?"

"Happy Father's Day."

"Thanks."

We unzip the tent, then work our way into our sleeping bags.

"Dad?"

"Yeah?"

"Was it a good one?"

"A good Father's Day? For sure. It was the best one ever."

"Really?"

"Of course, really."

"Oh."

We curl in close for warmth.

"Does that surprise you?" I ask.

"A little."

"Well, it shouldn't."

"Why?"

"Because you made me a book! Because we're camping alongside the ocean! Because we had pudding for dinner! We have so much, man. So much to be grateful for."

"Yeah," he says, closing his eyes. "I forgot about the pudding."

36. Henry's illustration of the ocean. Courtesy of the author.

12 Reflecting Light

The environs of our new home, surrounded by giant Fir trees, the
healthful sea breezes, the strange sights and sounds were sources of
continual thought. The long distance that separated us from our old
home in the Mississippi valley, precluded any form of home sickness
and our united efforts were wholly set upon the building of a home.

—Sarah Cummins, 1845

MONDAY, JUNE 18–TUESDAY, JUNE 19
WEATHER: MID-60S
RATIONS: BEACH PIZZA; AIRPORT BURRITOS
NEHALEM OR → EAU CLAIRE WI

Because all good things must come to an end, it does.

We are ready.

After our post-breakfast tooth brushing, we walk through the
campsite noting further proof of what we'd previously observed at
the Grand Island KOA in Doniphan, Nebraska: an unspoken one-
upmanship of whose got the biggest RV, the farthest-reaching satellite
dish, the most square footage of turf carpet. To our right a man flips
pancakes on an electric griddle, while a woman to his left appears
to be poaching an egg. I wouldn't be surprised to find an Orange
Julius stand sprouting from the landscape or, more likely, from the
back of someone's motor home.

Adding to this unseemly abundance of riches is the menagerie of
coolers. Apparently, every self-respecting camper (which excludes us)
maintains a dry cooler, a wet cooler, an ice cream cooler, a condiments

cooler, and a cooler into which the other coolers are stored. (You know, in case one of the aforementioned coolers springs a leak.)

All of which is to say: the phrase "roughing it" has no place here.

As our camping brethren take pains to determine who's got the best gear, I take pride in knowing that Henry and I have the worst. Not only do we lack a satellite dish and a griddle, but over the course of two thousand–plus miles, we've been forced to make do with a single disposable cooler, which is currently home to our hiking boots.

In terms of silverware we have one spork each.

In terms of poached eggs we have none.

What we do have—and what all those other folks are missing while realigning their satellite dishes—is the ocean, which on this cool Oregon morning belongs solely to us.

Because the clouds have yet to burn away, we don our sweatshirts, keeping the goose bumps at arm's length. Jogging toward the cliff to our right, Henry stops to grab a stick to scrawl our names in the sand. Though if we're trying to leave our mark behind, we've picked the wrong canvas; the tide makes short work of his etching.

Frustrated, Henry presses the stick to the sand a second time with the same result. In some ways this complicates our attempt to "make every mile a memory," though in other ways it reinforces the need for the memory. By losing the physical proof of our being there, what choice do we have but to remember?

Chucking the stick, Henry changes the subject.

"Hey Dad," he says, "race you to the cliff?"

"On three," I say. "One, two . . ."

I leave a step early.

"Hey, no fair!"

"Welcome to life!"

He laughs, screams, runs faster.

* * *

At a picnic table on the shores of the Nehalem River, Henry and I await our basket of fish and chips. For the last hour we've wandered the streets of Nehalem (population 292), in search of the perfect restaurant. In the end we settle on the Riverside Fish & Chips food truck parked alongside the river. We're suckers for a good view. Also: for fish and chips.

Henry retrieves our food from the truck window, walking it carefully to our picnic table on the backside of an antique store. Reaching for the lemon wedge, Henry douses the fried cod with a burst of citrus.

"Mmm . . . ," he says, flecks of fish shooting from his mouth. "Now that's good fish."

"Better than a handful of granola at Fort Kearny?"

"Mm-hmm."

"Better than a warm peanut butter sandwich at Scotts Bluff?"

"Oh yeah."

Across the river some bird I've never seen lifts like a kite toward a tree, disappearing into the foliage. On our side of the shore I spot a pair of purple flowers.

Ahead of us all we see is nature, while behind us all we see is town.

"Tomorrow at this time," I say, "we'll be in the Portland airport preparing to board."

"Really?" Henry says, dragging a French fry through a pool of ketchup. "That seems an awful long way from here."

"It does."

Peering out at those flowers, Henry says, "Mom and Eleanor are going to be so excited to see us."

"I'm pretty excited to see them too."

Henry nods, reaching for his fish.

"Though they probably won't even recognize you," I continue. "You've changed a lot."

"Yeah," he agrees. "Like, I read more books now. Not to brag, but I could probably read that whole joke book by myself now."

"And *Sideways Stories from Wayside School* too."

"Oh yeah!"

"Plus, you're more responsible now," I say. "You even know how to set up the tent."

More nodding.

"And sometimes," I say, a smile slipping across my face, "you even know how to screw the cap on a water bottle!"

"Sometimes," he says. "But don't worry, Dad. Sometimes I still need your help."

★ ★ ★

After lunch we wander the antique store directly behind us. Almost immediately, I strike up a conversation with Barbara, the woman working the cash register. She's a Seattle transplant who, a few years back, moved to Nehalem to escape city life.[1]

"I spent a good chunk of my career in a cubicle," Barbara tells me. "And once I retired, I knew I never wanted to go back to a place like that again." She works part-time at the antique store ("Just helping out a friend"), and when she asks what brings Henry and me to town, I give her the spiel.

"You mean you drove the *whole* Oregon Trail?" she asks.

"We did," I say.

"You know, my great grandma on my mother's side traveled the Oregon Trail too. She lived on the East Coast. She worked as a nanny for a political family. Then she got pregnant with the mister's baby," Barbara tells me, lowering her voice to a whisper. "She had money put in her hand, and then she was put on a train."

My eyes widen as I run through a list of era-specific East Coast politicians: Millard Fillmore, Franklin Pierce, James Buchanan. (Turns out they were all pretty much East Coasters back then.)

"Originally, we thought that meant a *locomotive* train, but in fact, she was put on a wagon train," Barbara continues. "And by the time she arrived out here, she had enough money to buy property in Tacoma, Washington."

"Do you remember her name?" I ask, desperate for clues.

"Not offhand," Barbara says. "And she was sworn to secrecy anyway."

Despite my detective work, I'll never uncover the story of the lovechild between Barbara's great-grandmother and the unnamed East Coast politician. But the tale's a reminder that people traveled west for all sorts of reasons. Much like Henry and me, sometimes they were running toward something, other times running away.

"Thanks for talking with me," I tell Barbara as our conversation winds down. "Through our trip Henry and I've learned so much just by talking to strangers. I don't know why you all talk to us, but I'm glad you do."

"Well, when you give off light, it reflects back," Barbara says simply. "And when it does, you have to be ready to receive it."

In all our chats with folks, I'd forgotten that we were always sharing parts of ourselves too. That more often than not, we gave and received in equal measure.

"Well, thanks," I say, a bit embarrassed. "I guess I never thought about it like that."

Henry meets me at the cash register, a toy in tow.

"Remember the money that lady at the bookstore gave me?" he asks.

I reach for my wallet and hand him Liz's five-dollar bill, which he turns over to Barbara.

"Good choice," she says, handing me the change. "And since you're here and all," she continues, reaching toward a basket of sand dollars, "let me give you fellas a couple of these to go."

She places a pair of sand dollars into a small bag.

"Thanks," I smile.

She nods, reflects it back.

★ ★ ★

Back at the beach, we go for one last walk. Henry spots piles of driftwood in the distance and decides he needs to make a fort. As we approach, however, we see that someone's beaten us to it. These aren't piles of driftwood but a tiny village of wooden, domed huts constructed between water and beach grass. We duck inside each of them, commenting on their size and durability and enjoying the way the sun streams through the empty spaces before settling like tiger stripes across our skin.

Though we enjoy our driftwood village interloping, sometime around 4:00 p.m. I say the inevitable: "Well bud, I think it's time we head back."

He's startled by the proposition.

"You mean . . . home?"

"Soon," I say, "but for now I just mean back to the tent."

37. Arrival at the Pacific Ocean, Nehalem Bay State Park, Nehalem, Oregon. Courtesy of the author.

"Oh," he says. "For a minute I thought you meant head back home."

Pause.

"But . . . I do want to go home," he admits.

"Me too."

Though we'd have never admitted it earlier, by our second to last day, home is the only destination we desire.

After all these days and all these miles, at last we have run out of things to talk about. No more lessons to tender or receive. No more adventures to embark upon. The sea air provides temporary relief, but it is a hard blow nonetheless: the knowledge that our road has temporarily run out. Our boundary momentarily stopped.

In the dunes just ahead, I see the trail leading toward our campsite.

"One last look at the ocean," I say, turning toward it. "Take a mental picture!"

We lift our imaginary cameras to our eyes.

Click.

No sooner do we commit this moment to memory than the memory changes. Overhead I hear a squall, and upon lifting my gaze, I lay eyes upon the most clichéd creature this moment could possibly have conjured. Here, at the end of our journey to "rediscover America," we see a bald eagle soaring majestically.

"Are you kidding me?" I shout, waving my arms. "Eagle, are you even for real?"

Surely this bird has been pulled from central casting—a near-perfect end to a near-perfect trip. I shake my head at the wonder of it all. How, in moments like this, the world is simply too much.

As the eagle concludes its air show and fades into the horizon, Henry turns to me.

"Dad?" he says.

"Yes, son?" I say.

"I think . . ."

Pause.

"You think what?"

"I think . . . ," he stammers.

"Buddy, it's okay, you can tell me."

This is the moment we've been waiting for. Not some eagle soaring, manufactured made-for-TV moment, but the one in which my unconditional love for my son is made clear to him and his is made clear to me. This is the moment that will forever bind us to some unknown plane, one half as high as Heaven and twice as deep as the Platte.

Henry looks at me, drawing upon his wellspring of strength.

"Well, I just think . . ."

"Yes?"

"I think . . . I'm finally . . . sick of you."

I smile, sigh, slap an arm around his not-so-small shoulder.

"You know, bud," I say, "I think I'm finally sick of you too."

We laugh because it's easier than the other thing.

★ ★ ★

That night we drive to the beach town of Manzanita for our last supper. The place welcomes us with the smell of pizza; what choice do we have but to order a large to go?

Twenty minutes later Henry's holding the box with outstretched arms, turning left and right to make sure the coast is clear before crossing the road toward the beach. We collapse in the sand just a stone's throw from the water, lifting the cardboard flap to find the still-sizzling pizza within. Gluttons that we are, we gobble it down in minutes, folding our slices in half just to speed up the process.

Midway through the pizza, we spot a couple in their sixties off to our right. They dawdle toward us, as if unsure whether or not to engage us in conversation. I smile, nod, try to shine a little light in their direction in an effort to lure them in.

I prepare myself for the question we've so often been asked throughout our trip: "What brings you fellas here?"

I've got the elevator pitch on the tip of my tongue, but they don't ask the question.

Instead, the woman smiles at us as they pass by.

"You know," she says, "that looks about perfect."

I'm not sure if she's talking about the pizza or the moment.

Either way she's right.

★ ★ ★

At dawn we collapse the tent one last time. We stuff our sleeping bags into sacks and roll our sleeping pads tight. But upon trying to shove our laundry bags into our suitcases, one fact becomes clear: there is no way in hell everything's coming back with us. For twelve days we'd turned Bullseye into our ever-expanding messy room, and now we're paying the price.

What to do with the damp clothes and the towels? With the spare shoes and the first-aid kit? Where can we stuff our fire hazard of a paper trail—the pamphlets, the maps, and the mini golf scores? According to airline regulations, all of this must fit within a couple of bags, and at 6:00 a.m., as Henry and I stare at the impossible task before us, we're quick to raise the white flag.

"Well," I say, "I think we'll have to make some hard decisions."

Because we can't bear to pitch it all, we pile the "good stuff" on the picnic table belonging to our camp neighbors—a pair of women we'd befriended the night before. We'd shared s'mores together, then offered them a few of the items I knew had no place on a plane: water, matches, bug spray, and sunscreen. By morning's light it's clear we have plenty more to give. I pile ponchos and the first-aid kit atop the women's picnic table.

Either it is a kindness or I have given them garbage—who can say for sure?

When Henry and I buckle up, Bullseye feels eerily empty. For the first time since our first day, everything is in its right place. We have replaced our helter-skelter scatter with feng shui simplicity. Our backpacks are zipped, our water bottles filled, and the accumulated sand and dirt from all our miles have been shaken from the floor mats.

Though we are just a hundred miles from the Portland airport, you wouldn't know it by the winding, tree-lined roads that lie ahead. Henry folds his hands in his lap, settling in for the final leg.

"All set?" I ask, pressing the ignition button.

Henry gives me his sleepy smile. And then dreams.

★ ★ ★

It happens in an instant: one minute we're pulling our bags from Bullseye's back seat, and the next minute he's gone. The man working the Portland airport's car rental return scribbles an indecipherable message on the Jeep's back window, then motions us out of the vehicle.

Had the opportunity presented itself, I would've hugged that Jeep Compass right then and there. Would've pressed my stubbly cheek to his dusty hood and said: "Thank you, old friend! May we cross paths on the next journey!"

For the past thirteen days Bullseye has been there for all of it. Who can forget the time he killed that bird with his windshield? Or the night we rode out the storm in his seats? He'd asked so little of us—a little gas, a little oil—and, in exchange, faithfully delivered us to safety.

"Come on, Dad," Henry says, reaching for my hand, "it's time to go."

38. Expressing our gratitude for Bullseye, somewhere in Oregon. Courtesy of the author.

But I don't go. Mostly, because I can't shake the feeling that Bullseye deserves better from us. Sentimental sucker that I am, I take a few deep breaths in that parking garage, trying to devise a more appropriate send-off.

But after being the target of a few sharp honks, I realize that I'm the one being sent off. Rather unceremoniously.

Taking the hint, I grab my bags and let Henry lead us out of there. But before we go, I turn once more to spot Bullseye being driven back to his corral.

"Ride like the wind, Bullseye!" I shout.

"Riiiiiiide like the wiiiiiind!" Henry cries.

* * *

Within weeks I'll forget all about the sand in the tent. And the bugs. And the wet firewood. And the smushed bread. And the damp towels. And the mold on the campground's bathroom floor. Instead, I'll only remember mourning doves. And fireflies. And the cool wind that cuts through Oregon's trees.

I have my selective memory to thank. A selective memory, I'll add, that was buoyed by my occasionally poor note-taking skills. Some nights I was simply too tired to document all our difficulties. As a result, it's as if those difficulties never occurred.

Later, while reviewing my notes, I'll notice one phrase that appears repeatedly, even on the sparsest note-taking days.

So. Much. Laughter.

★ ★ ★

Shortly after touchdown, while standing on the curb at the Minneapolis–Saint Paul International Airport, we're still laughing.

"Hey," Henry grins, squinting into the dark, "what if Mom forgets to pick us up?"

"She might forget to pick *me* up," I say, "but she'd never forget you."

Thankfully, both scenarios are disproved within minutes.

"Well, hey there!" Meredith calls, pulling the minivan to the curb. "Looking for a ride, strangers?"

Eleanor, in the back seat, lifts her hands as high as her car seat straps allow.

Since traffic refuses to halt on our behalves, we begin a mad dash of chucking bags into the trunk, strapping booster seats into buckles, and hugging and kissing the only people that Henry and I love as much as each other.

Instinctually, I hop in the driver's seat. We've barely peeled onto the highway before I'm abruptly reminded that our minivan is no Bullseye. Gone are the fancy doodads and gadgets to which we'd grown accustomed. Just like that, we're back to our no-frills life.

It's good to be back.

"Well," Meredith says, grasping Henry's hand. "Tell me all about it!"

"Tell us!" Eleanor says.

"I don't know," Henry shrugs, playing it cool. "It was all right, I guess."

"*Just* all right?" I ask.

"I don't know," he says, a faint smile brimming. "Pretty good."

The ninety miles from Minneapolis to Eau Claire pass just shy of eternity. When at last we pull into our driveway, it seems impossible that at the start of the day we were within rock-skipping distance of the ocean.

Loaded with luggage, we stumble into the living room to find our dog, Cici, heralding our return. She writhes and wiggles along the carpet, whimpering in what I like to believe is gratitude.

It is the closest to a hero's welcome we'll receive, and it's more than we deserve. We have done nothing heroic: just turned off some screens, made a few new friends, and marveled at a rock or two.

Climbing into bed that night, for the first time in a long time, I don't worry about tent stakes. Or rainflies. Or inclement weather. All I worry about is the world we're missing while tucked safely in our beds.

Placing my head on the cool side of the pillow, I think about Chimney Rock looming large in the Nebraskan moonlight. And of Scotts Bluff thrusting its rocky chin down toward the town. I think of the wind rattling our tent just outside of Casper. Of Joel Hembree's grave standing tall among the weeds. I think of Rebecca Winters and handcarts and hot springs and ice cream and an eagle cutting through the clouds over the Pacific. I think about flashlight beams in Montpelier. And the bar of soap we wore down to a sliver by trip's end. I think of the blue morpho butterfly in Boise. And the swales and the ruts from the wagons that came before. And of fried fish, purple flowers, sand dollars slipped in a bag. But mostly, I think about what Henry and I will never have again: such unencumbered togetherness.

And such love-fueled, laughter-filled ease.

"Well?" my wife whispers into the dark. "Was it everything you'd hoped?"

"More," I say, turning toward her. "It was everything and more."

NOTES

PROLOGUE
1. Steinbeck, *Travels with Charley.*
2. Franzwa, *Oregon Trail Revisited.*

1. THE JUMPING-OFF POINT
Epigraph: Eide, *Oregon Trail.*
1. "America the Beautiful: About the Song."
2. Hauptman, "Mythologizing Westward Expansion."
3. McGrath, *Art and the American Conservation Movement.*
4. McGrath, *Art and the American Conservation Movement.*
5. Thoreau, "Walking."
6. Barton, *One Woman's West.*
7. Schlissel, *Women's Diaries of the Westward Journey.*
8. Schlissel, *Women's Diaries of the Westward Journey.*
9. Barton, *One Woman's West.*
10. Barton, *One Woman's West.*
11. Barton, *One Woman's West.*
12. Barton, *One Woman's West.*
13. Barton, *One Woman's West.*
14. Barton, *One Woman's West.*
15. Wilder, *Little House on the Prairie.*

2. STUBBORN AS MULES
Epigraph: Eide, *Oregon Trail.*
1. Potter, *Trail to California.*
2. Ralph Goldsmith, personal interview, June 8, 2018.
3. Paden, *Wake of the Prairie Schooler.*

4. Mattes, *Great Platte River Road.*

5. Eide, *Oregon Trail.*

6. Goldsmith, interview.

7. Travis Boley, personal interview, June 8, 2018.

8. O'Sullivan, "Annexation."

9. Dunbar-Ortiz, *Indigenous Peoples' History of the United States.*

10. Unruh, *Plains Across.*

11. Duane Iles, personal interview, June 8, 2018.

12. Bryant, *What I Saw.*

13. Bryant, *What I Saw.*

14. Unruh, *Plains Across.*

3. WEATHERING THE STORM

Epigraph: Eide, *Oregon Trail.*

1. Franzwa, *Oregon Trail Revisited.*

2. Paden, *Wake of the Prairie Schooler.*

3. Meeker, *Ox Team.*

4. Eide, *Oregon Trail.*

5. Mattes, *Great Platte River Road.*

6. Mattes, *Great Platte River Road.*

7. Gene Hunt, personal interview, June 9, 2018.

8. Potter, *Trail to California.*

9. Mattes, *Great Platte River Road.*

10. Spencer, "Ogallaly, Queen of the Cow Towns."

11. Mary Cone, personal interview, June 9, 2018.

12. Vance and Karen Nelson, personal interview, June 9, 2018.

13. Don Rawitsch, personal interview, February 14, 2018.

4. FAITH AND CONSEQUENCES

Epigraph: Eide, *Oregon Trail.*

1. Eide, *Oregon Trail.*

2. Eide, *Oregon Trail.*

3. Eide, *Oregon Trail.*

4. Franzwa, *Oregon Trail Revisited.*

5. Eide, *Oregon Trail.*

6. Loren Pospisil, personal interview, June 10, 2018, and June 17, 2019.

7. U.S. National Park Service, "Rebecca Winters Story."

8. Roger Castle, personal interview, June 10, 2018.

9. Rachel Burr, personal interview, June 10, 2018.
10. Stegner, *Gathering of Zion*.
11. Eide, *Oregon Trail*.
12. Meldahl, *Hard Road West*.
13. Shumway, *History of Western Nebraska and Its People*.
14. "Platte Claims Another Victim."
15. U.S. National Park Service, "Fort Laramie."
16. Steve Fullmer, personal interview, June 10, 2018.
17. Wikipedia, "Treaty of Fort Laramie (1851)," last modified March 4, 2020, https://en.wikipedia.org/wiki/Treaty_of_Fort_Laramie_(1851).
18. Wikipedia, "Treaty of Fort Laramie (1868)," last modified November 28, 2018, https://en.wikipedia.org/wiki/Treaty_of_Fort_Laramie_(1868).
19. Nabokov, *Native American Testimony*.
20. Nabokov, *Native American Testimony*.
21. Nabokov, *Native American Testimony*.
22. Wikipedia, "Dawes Act," last modified May 27, 2020, https://en.wikipedia.org/wiki/Dawes_Act.
23. Fixico, "Ethics and Responsibilities in Writing American Indian History."
24. Brown, *Bury My Heart at Wounded Knee*.
25. Eide, *Oregon Trail*.
26. Potter, *Trail of California*.

5. PROCEED WITH CAUTION

Epigraph: Eide, *Oregon Trail*.
1. Oregon-California Trails Association, "Life and Death on the Oregon Trail."
2. Blair, "Doctor Gets Some Practice."
3. Franzwa, *Oregon Trail Revisited*.
4. Franzwa, *Oregon Trail Revisited*.
5. Blair, "Doctor Gets Some Practice."
6. Roger P. Blair, personal interview, March 5, 2018.
7. Franzwa, *Oregon Trail Revisited*.
8. Eide, *Oregon Trail*.
9. Franzwa, *Oregon Trail Revisited*.
10. Eide, *Oregon Trail*.

11. Wikipedia, "Bison," last modified March 1, 2019, https://en
.wikipedia.org/wiki/Bison.

12. Meeker, *Ox Team.*

13. Nabokov, *Native American Testimony.*

14. Nabokov, *Native American Testimony* (and for quotations that follow).

15. U.S. National Park Service, "Frequently Asked Questions: Bison."

16. Randy Brown, personal interview, June 11, 2018.

17. Winton, "William T. Newby's Diary of the Emigration of 1843."

18. Barton, *One Woman's West.*

19. Brown, interview; "Attack on the Kelly-Larimer Wagon Train."

6. RECALCULATING THE ROUTE

Epigraph: Eide, *Oregon Trail.*

1. Franzwa, *Oregon Trail Revisited.*

2. Meldahl, *Hard Road West.*

3. Berry, *World-Ending Fire.*

4. Wikipedia, "Mormon Handcart Pioneers," last modified December
25, 2018, https://en.wikipedia.org/wiki/Mormon_handcart_pioneers.

5. Stegner, *Gathering of Zion.*

6. Stegner, *Gathering of Zion.*

7. Wikipedia, "Mormon Handcart Pioneers."

8. Wikipedia, "Mormon Handcart Pioneers."

9. Hein, "Journey to Martin's Cove."

10. Moulton, *Mormon Handcart Migration.*

11. Moulton, *Mormon Handcart Migration.*

12. Wikipedia, "Mormon Trail," last modified June 10, 2020, https://en
.wikipedia.org/wiki/Mormon_Trail.

7. THE GHOSTS OF EMIGRANTS PAST

Epigraph: Eide, *Oregon Trail.*

1. Shawneen Wuthrich, personal interview, June 13, 2018.

2. Kale Wuthrich, personal interview, June 13, 2018.

3. Becky Smith, personal interview, June 13, 2018.

4. Wikipedia, "Bear River Massacre," last modified June 5, 2019,
https://en.wikipedia.org/wiki/Bear_River_Massacre.

5. Dimuro, "Forgotten Bear River Massacre"; Wikipedia, "Bear River Massacre."

6. Wikipedia, "Wounded Knee Massacre," last modified June 24,
2020, https://en.wikipedia.org/wiki/Wounded_Knee_Massacre;

Wikipedia, "Sand Creek Massacre," last modified June 23, 2020, https://en.wikipedia.org/wiki/Sand_Creek_massacre.

8. SMALL KINDNESSES

Epigraph: Eide, *Oregon Trail.*

1. Donner Houghton, *Expedition of the Donner Party and Its Tragic Fate.*
2. Werner, *Pioneer Children on the Journey West.*
3. Werner, *Pioneer Children on the Journey West.*
4. Donner Houghton, *Expedition of the Donner Party and Its Tragic Fate.*
5. Dave Johnson, personal interview, June 14, 2018.
6. Donner Houghton, *Expedition of the Donner Party and Its Tragic Fate.*

9. THE HOUSE ALWAYS WINS

Epigraph: Eide, *Oregon Trail.*

1. Sarah Lecompte, personal interview, June 15, 2018.
2. Wikipedia, "History of Human Migration," last modified February 25, 2019, https://en.wikipedia.org/wiki/History_of_human_migration.
3. Allyn, "Trail Experiences in 1853."
4. Allyn, "Trail Experiences in 1853."
5. John Bevis, personal interview, June 15, 2018, and June 12, 2019.
6. Unruh, *Plains Across.*
7. Unruh, *Plains Across.*
8. Brown, *Bury My Heart at Wounded Knee.*
9. Lewy, "Were American Indians the Victims of Genocide?"
10. Bevis, interview, June 12, 2019.

10. REDRAWING THE BOUNDARIES

Epigraph: Meeker, *Ox Team.*

1. Whitman, *Tamsen Donner.*
2. Wikipedia, "Portland," last modified March 6, 2019, https://en.wikipedia.org/wiki/Portland_Oregon.
3. Meeker, *Ox Team.*
4. O'Sullivan, "Annexation."
5. Liz Nakazawa, personal interview, June 16, 2018.
6. Ellie Isenhart, personal interview, June 16, 2018.

11. THE GIFT

Epigraph: Eide, *Oregon Trail.*

1. Unruh, *Plains Across*.
2. Unruh, *Plains Across*.
3. Unruh, *Plains Across*.
4. John Jarvie, personal interview, June 17, 2018.

12. REFLECTING LIGHT

Epigraph: Eide, *Oregon Trail*.
1. Barbara Clark, personal interview, June 18, 2018.

BIBLIOGRAPHY

Allyn, Henry. "Trail Experiences in 1853." In *With Her Own Wings: Historical Sketches, Reminiscences, and Anecdotes of Oregon's Pioneer Women,* edited by Helen Krebs Smith. Rockville MD: Wildside Press, 2008.

"America the Beautiful: About the Song." Ballad of America website. August 18, 2019. http://www.balladofamerica.com/music/indexes /songs/americathebeautiful/index.htm.

"Attack on the Kelly-Larimer Wagon Train." WyoHistory.org. January 17, 2016. https://www.wyohistory.org/encyclopedia/attack-kelly-larimer -wagon-train.

Barton, Lois, ed. *One Woman's West: Recollections of the Oregon Trail and Settling the Northwest Country by Martha Gay Masterson.* Eugene OR: Spencer Butte Press, 1986.

Berry, Wendell. *The World-Ending Fire: The Essential Wendell Berry.* Berkeley CA: Counterpoint, 2017.

Blair, Roger P. "The Doctor Gets Some Practice: Cholera and Medicine on the Overland Trails." *Journal of the West* 36, no. 1 (1997).

Brown, Dee. *Bury My Heart at Wounded Knee: An Indian History of the American West.* New York: Picador, 2000.

Buck, Rinker. *The Oregon Trail: A New American Journey.* New York: Simon & Schuster Paperbacks, 2015.

Burton, Gabrielle. *Searching for Tamsen Donner.* Lincoln: University of Nebraska Press, 2009.

Cronkite, Walter. *Around America: A Tour of Our Magnificent Coastline.* New York: W. W. Norton, 2001.

Debczak, Michael. "How Lewis Keseberg Was Branded the Killer Cannibal of the Donner Party." *Mental Floss,* September 19, 2018. Web. March 6, 2019.

DeVoto, Bernard, ed. *The Journals of Lewis and Clark.* Boston: Houghton Mifflin, 1981.

Dimuro, Gina. "The Forgotten Bear River Massacre May Be the Deadliest Native American Slaughter Ever." AllThatsInteresting.com. July 9, 2018. https://allthatsinteresting.com/bear-river-massacre.

Donner Houghton, Eliza P. *The Expedition of the Donner Party and Its Tragic Fate.* Lincoln: University of Nebraska Press, 1997.

Duffin, Reg P. "The Grave of Joel Hembree." *Overland Journal* 3, no. 2 (1985).

Dunbar-Ortiz, Roxanne. *An Indigenous Peoples' History of the United States.* New York: Beacon Press, 2015.

Eide, Ingvard Henry. *The Oregon Trail.* Chicago: Rand McNally, 1972.

Fanselow, Julie. *Traveling the Oregon Trail.* Guilford CT: Globe Pequot Press, 2001.

Fixico, Donald L. "Ethics and Responsibilities in Writing American Indian History." *American Indian Quarterly* 20, no. 1 (1996).

Franzwa, Gregory M. *The Oregon Trail Revisited.* Tucson: Patrice Press, 1997.

Frazier, Ian. *Great Plains.* New York: Farrar, Straus Giroux, 1989.

Hafen, Leroy R., and Ann W. Hafen. *Handcarts to Zion: The Story of a Unique Western Migration, 1856–1860.* Lincoln: University of Nebraska Press, 1992.

Haines, Aubrey L. *Historic Sites along the Oregon Trail.* Gerald MO: Patrice Press, 1981.

Hampsten, Elizabeth. *Settlers' Children: Growing Up on the Great Plains.* Norman: University of Oklahoma Press, 1991.

Handley, R. William, and Nathaniel Lewis, eds. *True West: Authenticity and the American West.* Lincoln: University of Nebraska Press, 2003.

Hauptman, Laurence M. "Mythologizing Westward Expansion: Schoolbooks and the Image of the American Frontier." *Western Historical Quarterly* 8, no. 3 (1977).

Hein, Annette. "Journey to Martin's Cove: The Mormon Handcart Tragedy of 1856." WyoHistory.org. November 8, 2014. https://www.wyohistory.org/encyclopedia/journey-martins-cove-mormon-handcart-tragedy-1856.

"Henry Dyer Nichols Drowned." *Mitchell Index,* August 7, 1908.

Hill, William E. *The Oregon Trail: Yesterday and Today.* Caldwell ID: Caxton Printers, Ltd., 1986.

Holmes, Kenneth L., ed. *Best of Covered Wagon Women.* Norman: University of Oklahoma Press, 2008.

Jeffrey, Julie Roy. *Frontier Women: The Trans-Mississippi West, 1840–1880.* New York: Hill & Wang, 1979.

"Joel Jasper Hembree." Find a Grave. https://www.findagrave.com /memorial/8332395/joel-jasper-hembree.

Katz, William Loren. *The Black West: A Documentary and Pictorial History of the African American Role in the Westward Expansion of the United States.* New York: Touchstone, 1996.

Landau, Elaine. *The Oregon Trail.* New York: Children's Press, 2006.

Langworthy, Franklin, and Paul C. Phillips, eds. *Scenery of the Plains, Mountains and Mines: Narratives of the Trans-Mississippi Frontier.* Princeton: Princeton University Press, 1932.

Lewy, Guenther. "Were American Indians the Victims of Genocide?" History News Network. September 2004. https://historynewsnetwork.org/article/7302.

Limerick, Patricia Nelson. *The Legacy of Conquest: The Unbroken Past of the American West.* New York: W. W. Norton, 1987.

Mattes, Merrill J. *The Great Platte River Road.* Lincoln: University of Nebraska Press, 1987.

McDermott, John Francis, ed. *An Artist on the Overland Trail: The 1849 Diary and Sketches of James F. Wilkins.* San Marino CA: Huntington Library, 1968.

McGlashan, C. F. *History of the Donner Party: A Tragedy of the Sierras.* Sacramento: H. S. Crocker Co., Printers, 1907.

McGrath, Robert L. *Art and the American Conservation Movement.* Boston: National Park Service, U.S. Department of the Interior, 2001.

Mead, Margaret. *And Keep Your Powder Dry: An Anthropologist Looks At America.* New York: William Morrow, 1943.

Meeker, Ezra. *The Ox Team; or, The Old Oregon Trail, 1852–1906.* New York: n.p., 1907.

Meldahl, Keith Heyer. *Hard Road West.* Chicago: University of Chicago Press, 2007.

Monaghan, Jay, ed. *The Book of the American West.* New York: Simon & Schuster, 1963.

Morgan, Robert. *Lions of the West: Heroes and Villains of the Westward Expansion.* Chapel Hill NC: Algonquin Books, 2012.

Moulton, Candy. *The Mormon Handcart Migration: "Tounge nor Pen Can Never Tell the Sorrow."* Norman: University of Oklahoma Press, 2019.

Musolf, Nell. *The Split History of Westward Expansion in the United States.* Stevens Point WI: Compass Point Books, 2013.

Nabokov, Peter, ed. *Native American History: A Chronicle of Indian-White Relations from Prophecy to the Present, 1492–1992.* New York: Viking, 1991.

Needleman, Jacob. *The American Soul: Rediscovering the Wisdom of Our Founders.* New York: Jeremy P. Tarcher / Putnam, 2002.

Oregon-California Trails Association. "Life and Death on the Oregon Trail." https://www.octa-trails.org/articles/life-and-death-on-the -oregon-trail/.

O'Sullivan, John. "Annexation." *Democratic Review* 17, no. 1 (July–August 1845). https://pdcrodas.webs.ull.es/anglo/OSullivanAnnexation .pdf.

Paden, Irene D. *The Wake of the Prairie Schooner.* New York: Macmillan, 1943.

Page, Elizabeth. *Wagons West: A Story of the Oregon Trail.* New York: Farrar and Rinehart, 1930.

Palmer, Rosemary Gudmundson. *Children's Voices from the Trail: Narratives of the Platte River Road.* Spokane WA: Arthur H. Clark Co., 2002.

Parkman, Francis. *The Oregon Trail.* New York: Signet Classic, 1978.

Peavy, Linda, and Ursula Smith. *Frontier Children.* Norman: University of Oklahoma Press, 1999.

"The Platte Claims Another Victim." *Morrill Mail,* August 1908.

Potter, David M., ed. *Trail to California: The Overland Journal of Vincent Geiger and Wakeman Bryarly.* New Haven CT: Yale University Press, 1962.

Rarick, Ethan. *Desperate Passage: The Donner Party's Perilous Journey West.* Oxford: Oxford University Press, 2008.

Ridge, Martin, ed. *Frederick Jackson Turner: Wisconsin's Historian of the Frontier.* Madison: State Historical Society of Wisconsin, 1986.

Rosenberg, Charles E. *The Cholera Years: The United States in 1832, 1849, and 1866.* Chicago: University of Chicago Press, 2009.

Schlissel, Lillian. *Women's Diaries of the Westward Journey.* New York: Schocken Books, 1982.

Shumway, Grant Lee. *History of Western Nebraska and Its People.* Lincoln NE: Western Publishing and Engraving Co., 1921.

Slotkin, Richard. *Regeneration through Violence: The Mythology of the American Frontier, 1600–1860.* Middletown CT: Wesleyan University Press, 1973.

Spencer, Matthew. "Ogallaly, Queen of the Cow Towns." *Nebraska Life Magazine*, January–February 2013.

Stefoff, Rebecca. *The Oregon Trail in American History*. Springfield NJ: Enslow Publishers, 1997.

Stegner, Wallace. *The Gathering of Zion: The Story of the Mormon Trail*. Lincoln NE: Bison Books, 1992.

Steinbeck, John. *Travels with Charley: In Search of America*. New York: Penguin Books, 2002.

Stewart, George R. *Ordeal by Hunger*. London: Jonathan Cape, 1936.

Strayed, Cheryl. *Wild: From Lost to Found on the Pacific Crest Trail*. New York: Alfred A. Knopf, 2012.

Tappan, William. "William Tappan's Diary, 1848." Nebraska Studies.org. http://d1vmz9rl3e2j4x.cloudfront.net/nebstudies/0403_0702tappan .pdf.

Terrie, Philip G. "The Other Within: Indianization on the Oregon Trail." *New England Quarterly* 64, no. 3 (1991).

Thoreau, Henry David. "Walking." *Atlantic*, June 1862.

Unruh, John D., Jr. *The Plains Across: The Overland Emigrants and the Trans-Mississippi West, 1840–60*. Urbana: University of Illinois Press, 1979.

U.S. National Park Service. Fort Laramie. "Fort Laramie: Crossings of a Nation Moving West." 2015. https://www.nps.gov/fola/learn /historyculture/index.htm.

———. "Frequently Asked Questions: Bison." https://www.nps.gov/yell /learn/nature/bisonfaq.htm.

———. "The Rebecca Winters Story." https://www.nps.gov/scbl /planyourvisit/upload/rebecca-winters-story.pdf.

Vance, James E. "The Oregon Trail and Union Pacific Railroad: A Contrast in Purpose." *Annals of the Association of American Geographers* 51, no. 4 (1961). www.jstor.org/stable/2561339.

Wallis, Michael. *The Best Land under Heaven: The Donner Party in the Age of Manifest Destiny*. New York: Liveright, 2017.

Werner, Emmy E. *Pioneer Children on the Journey West*. Boulder CO: Westview Press, 1995.

West, Elliot. *Growing Up with the Country: Childhood on the Far Western Frontier*. Albuquerque: University of New Mexico Press, 1989.

Whitman, Ruth. *Tamsen Donner: A Woman's Journey*. Cambridge MA: Alice James Books, 1977.

Wilder, Laura Ingalls. *Little House on the Prairie.* New York: HarperCollins, 1953.

Winton, Harry N. M. "William T. Newby's Diary of the Emigration of 1843." *Oregon Historical Quarterly* 40, no. 3 (1939). Web. May 19, 2019.

Wright, Sylvia. "The Search Is On for the Site of the Worst Indian Massacre in U.S. History." Smithsonian.com. May 13, 2016. https://www.smithsonianmag.com/history/search-site-worst-indian-massacre-us-history-180959091/.